On Military Science: A Guide to Understanding the Meaning of F.O.I. (Volume 3)

By Mikaeel D. Shabazz Muhammad

On Military Science: A Guide to Understanding the Meaning of F.O.I. (Volume 3)
Copyright 2012
By Mikaeel D. Shabazz Muhammad
ISBN 978-0-578-10492-8

Dedication

This volume is dedicated to my lovely wife Stephanie whom I love (and am in love with) immeasurably. It cannot be expressed in fair enough words how her love, support, faith in me, and patience with me, helped make this work possible, all three volumes included. She is truly the other half of my faith in Islam and the crown jewel of my heart and I am forever thankful, grateful, and appreciative that Allah (God) blessed me with the most wonderful woman a man could have in his corner and in his life.

> "*And We sent not before thee any but men to whom We sent revelation – so ask the followers of the Reminder if you know not – With clear arguments and Scriptures. And We have revealed to thee the Reminder that thou mayest make clear to men that which has been revealed to them, and that haply they may reflect.*"
> – **Holy Qur'an**, Surah 16:43-44

Preface

Supreme Wisdom, Saviors and Redeemers

The Supreme Wisdom, in the instructions to the Laborers (of the Nation of Islam), says *"You must qualify yourselves for positions awaiting you."* Positions "awaiting" implies something in store for you, not necessarily something already set up, therefore it can not possibly be limited to the established laboring positions of Minister, Captain, Secretary. These were positions set up in the infancy of the Nation of Islam over 80 years ago. In many organizations during the 1950's to the 1970's, the Nation of Islam included, under the counter-intelligence program (COINTELPRO) of the Federal Bureau of Investigations, led by then director J. Edgar Hoover, said organizations were monitored, infiltrated, disrupted, sabotaged, misrepresented, and then some. These organizations which attempted to address the needs of the poor, disenfranchised masses of people of color in the United States were accused of being communist sympathizers, anti-American, and such, while the U.S. government was busy disrupting foreign governments, destabilizing their infrastructures, usurping their resources, assassinating (and attempting to assassinate) so-called "dictators" and outright lying to the masses of the people about the motives for their involvement in World War II, the Korean War, Vietnam, Cuba, Laos, Cambodia,...and the list goes on. Be mindful that the COINTELPRO was successfully kept a secret until 1971! It was the Citizens Commission to Investigate the FBI, a leftist activist group, whose members broke into an FBI office in Media, Pennsylvania, March 8, 1971, stealing over 1000 classified documents and anonymously mailing them to several newspapers throughout the country, thus exposing us to the CONTELPRO. The first complete set of these documents wasn't published until March of 1972, and no major investigation of these classified documents or the FBI's activities were conducted until 1976 (AFTER the Messenger's departure and the break-up of the NOI). While the FBI, under then director J. Edgar Hoover, "officially" terminated their COINTELPRO activities, by NO means did it end after this announcement.

The Most Hon. Elijah Muhammad and the Nation of Islam were specifically mentioned as primary targets in a 1968 communiqué from J. Edgar Hoover on March 4th, just one month before the assassination of Dr. Martin Luther King, Jr. and not quite a month after the Most Hon. Elijah Muhammad sat and talked with Dr. M.L. King at the Palace in Chicago. It is from this communiqué that J. Edgar Hoover's long-range goals were expressed. My question is have these long-range goals been carried out even after the FBI's COINTELPRO was allegedly shut down by Mr. Hoover one month after the classified documents were taken from that Media, Pennsylvania 2-man FBI office? The document[1] outlining the COINTELPRO's long-range goals is as follows:

---

[1] As can be viewed on http://whatreallyhappened.com/RANCHO/POLITICS/COINTELPRO/COINTELPRO-FBI.docs.html

[...]

GOALS
~~~~~

For maximum effectiveness of the Counterintelligence Program, and to prevent wasted effort, long-range goals are being set.

1. Prevent the COALITION of militant black nationalist groups. In unity there is strength; a truism that is no less valid for all its triteness. An effective coalition of black nationalist groups might be the first step toward a real "Mau Mau" [Black revolutionary army] in America, the beginning of a true black revolution.

2. Prevent the rise of a "MESSIAH" who could unify, and electrify, the militant black nationalist movement. Malcolm X might have been such a "messiah;" he is the martyr of the movement today. Martin Luther King, Stokely Carmichael and Elijah Muhammed all aspire to this position. Elijah Muhammed is less of a threat because of his age. King could be a very real contender for this position should he abandon his supposed "obedience" to "white, liberal doctrines" (nonviolence) and embrace black nationalism. Carmichael has the necessary charisma to be a real threat in this way.

3. Prevent VIOLENCE on the part of black nationalist groups. This is of primary importance, and is, of course, a goal of our investigative activity; it should also be a goal of the Counterintelligence Program to pinpoint potential troublemakers and neutralize them before they exercise their potential for violence.

4. Prevent militant black nationalist groups and leaders from gaining RESPECTABILITY, by discrediting them to three separate segments of the community. The goal of discrediting black nationalists must be handled tactically in three ways. You must discredit those groups and individuals to, first, the responsible Negro community. Second, they must be discredited to the white community, both the responsible community and to "liberals" who have vestiges of sympathy for militant black nationalist [sic] simply because they are Negroes. Third, these groups must be discredited in the eyes of Negro radicals, the followers of the movement. This last area requires entirely different tactics from the first two. Publicity about violent tendencies and radical statements merely enhances black nationalists to the last group; it adds "respectability" in a different way.

5. A final goal should be to prevent the long-range GROWTH of militant black organizations, especially among youth. Specific tactics to prevent these groups from converting young people must be developed. [...]

TARGETS
~~~~~~~

Primary targets of the Counterintelligence Program, Black Nationalist-Hate Groups, should be the most violent and radical groups and their leaders. We should emphasize those leaders and organizations that are nationwide in scope and are most capable of disrupting this country. These targets, members, and followers of the:

   Student Nonviolent Coordinating Committee (SNCC)
   Southern Christian Leadership Conference (SCLC)
   Revolutionary Action Movement (RAM)
   Nation of Islam (NOI)

Offices handling these cases and those of Stokely Carmichael of SNCC, H. Rap Brown of SNCC, Martin Luther King of SCLC, Maxwell Stanford of RAM, and Elijah Muhammed of NOI, should be alert for counterintelligence suggestions.

Re-examining the more than 1,000 classified documents exposed from the FBI is a must. The tactics used in the proposed "long-range goals" of former FBI Director J. Edgar Hoover seem to have been "set" in the heart of every so-called "militant black nationalist group" of Hoover's era, even today. We cannot be foolish enough to believe that the Nation of Islam, which was one of these groups named directly along with the Most Hon. Elijah Muhammad, re-emerged under the guidance and leadership of the Hon. Louis Farrakhan free and clear of the machinations of the long-range goals proposed by Mr. Hoover, et al. This is why I referred much to what I call "Agents of Ignorance (AI)" in my previous volumes of 'On Military Science', because it seems that when we look at where we SHOULD be as a Nation and where we ARE, there can be no doubt that we have been subjected to these same aims and goals of the COINTELPRO, knowingly or unknowingly, willingly or unwillingly. We have been damaged by *coalition*-sabotage, preventing us from joining on effectively with other progressive organizations to bring about needed changes. Only Allah has had His hand and hedge over and around the Hon. Louis Farrakhan, so the enemy has been unsuccessful at preventing the rise of a black "messiah" who could unify and electrify the masses (recall the Million Man March and any other gathering called by the Hon. Louis Farrakhan). However, we have still been damaged by the sabotage of our organization and leadership in gaining *respectability* due to the actions of our own ignorance and foolish actions coupled with the actions of these unknown agent saboteurs. And we must also realize that the final long-range goal of J. Edgar Hoover which was preventing our *long-range growth*, as the NOI was a primary target, and they especially sought special tactics to prevent the youth from "converting." As we look at the condition of our youth today (both within and outside the NOI) there is no doubt that these "special tactics" were indeed developed and effective.

Yet, and still, there is and are solutions, but it requires us to become, in deed and fact as well as in name, true Saviors and Redeemers of our people as the Fruit of Islam. And so the Hon. Louis Farrakhan's words from 'The Meaning of F.O.I.' are even truer and more applicable today than when they were spoken and transcribed that:

"...the word of God coming through you will save anybody who will listen to you if you will study and qualify yourself for your work as a Saviour of our people." - Hon. Louis Farrakhan, 'Meaning of F.O.I.' (page 6)

"A Redeemer is one who is willing to pay a price to redeem someone or something that he loves." - Hon. Louis Farrakhan, 'Meaning of F.O.I.' (page 7)

Redeem means to "restore value to" something or someone. It is still a fascination for most men to see older model cars that have been restored to pristine condition. Anyone who has ever restored a classic car or older model car could spend hours discussing the fine details of what has been done to restore/redeem the car and how much money and man-hours were spent in doing so. Any car enthusiast would gladly sit and listen as well. And the odd thing about it that no one may have considered is that the value of a classic automobile that has been restored/redeemed to excellent condition is worth more than it was when it originally came off the factory line, ESPECIALLY WHEN "ORIGINAL" PARTS ARE USED.

How much more value will we have when we are redeemed and work to save and redeem our people and restore them back to their "original" selves, teaching and training them how to accept their own and be themselves? In my opinion, it is military training that is needed to do just that, and military training has proven to be transformative in nature and through the right type of military training. I'm speaking of that kind of military training that reflects what the Hon. Louis Farrakhan said beginning on page 19 of '*The Meaning of F.O.I.*':

"We are righteous men, with a righteous purpose, and if we are opposed in carrying out that righteous purpose, we will fight like hell with those who fight with us, in the name of Allah, and we will whip the hell out of any that come against us, short or tall, armed or unarmed. But we got to be right with our God. I hope this is clear now. And when you move out, move out as soldiers, but not as the devil's soldiers. Whose soldiers are we? Muhammad's! Which Muhammad? The Honorable Elijah Muhammad! Well, He is a Saviour of Black people. What about you? He paid a price to redeem the Black man. What about you? Come on brothers. If we're soldiers for Muhammad, let's get after his people.

Take this, study it, compare it with all you have studied of the Messenger and you will know that everything that I have said is 100% the truth and you must be trained in that manner or you will not be accepted by Allah and the Messenger as a part of the Fruit of Islam. Thank you."

And I thank you for picking up Volume 3 of '*On Military Science: A Guide to Understanding the Meaning of F.O.I.*' as this series was indeed inspired by that little book with POWERFUL words by the Hon. Louis Farrakhan, '*The Meaning of F.O.I.*' And I sincerely pray that Allah (God) blesses you with something of substance from this material to help us all become better servants of God and of better service to humanity through the study and application of military science and any other science we can use to accomplish such.

Your brother,
Harder on the Devil than a thousand ignorant worshipers,
Mikaeel. D. Shabazz Muhammad

On Military Science: A Guide to Understanding the Meaning of F.O.I. (Volume 3)

Table of Contents

Section 1

Last Letters to Southern Region Officers

"...if the HEM who was among us, laying a foundation for us to work today, has now left our midst but deposited in us his word and the same course of study that Master Fard Muhammad gave him, then why should we study? It is because you must study to save and deliver the people." – Hon. Louis Farrakhan, *'The Meaning of F.O.I.'* (pg 5)

Chapter 1

If We Would But Read, Knowledge, Applied Faith, and Education (Parts 1 and 2)

Dec. 17, 2011

"The feeling of commiseration is the beginning of humanity; the feeling of shame and dislike is the beginning of righteousness; the feeling of deference and compliance is the beginning of propriety; and the feeling of right or wrong is the beginning of wisdom. Men have these Four Beginnings just as they have their four limbs. Having these four beginnings, but saying that they cannot develop them is to destroy themselves."

- Mencius (also known as Meng-tzu)

As salaam alaikum,

As I had just published volume 2 of my book *'On Military Science: A Guide to Understanding the Meaning of F.O.I.'* I thought over the "functionally illiterate" masses of people (within the NOI as well) who are destroyed for a lack of knowledge because, as the bible says, they reject knowledge. This may be the reason why there are those who have not gravitated towards the Dianetics technology the Hon. Louis Farrakhan urged us to take on, because it requires not only reading but a demonstration of reading comprehension. I found the above quote while researching an ancient Chinese philosopher named Mencius. Mencius was a student of Taoism and a devout student and defender of the teachings of Confucius. Mencius spoke more in depth on human nature and asserted the innate goodness of the individual, believing that it was society's influence (society's lack of a positive cultivating influence) that caused bad moral character. *"He who exerts his mind to the utmost knows his nature"* and *"the way of learning is none other than finding the lost mind,"* are just a couple of quotes of his translated from the Chinese language around 300 B.C. Do these quotes sound familiar? Is this not an axiom of L.R. Hubbard that all of humanity (man) is inherently good? And you think Mr. Hubbard just came up with that and other such axioms uninfluenced by ancient teachings of past scholars?

When we don't study history or historical figures we cheat ourselves of understanding the origin of things. And this is why we fail to understand the nature of things, and why we suffer from the aggregate failures of learning, anticipation, and adaptation, as too many of us remain functionally illiterate. The Most Hon. Elijah Muhammad said that when you study the circumstances surrounding the birth or origin of a thing you can determine the nature of that thing. In the **Supreme Wisdom Lost-Found Muslim Lesson No. 1** the question is asked *"Why does the Devil keep our people illiterate? ANS. - So that he can use them for a tool, also a slave.[1]"* And today we have access to the information superhighway (internet) as well as access to libraries and book stores and yet, though we are physically free the majority of our minds (in the NOI) remain poor students with poor study habits. Was not the FIRST revelation to the Prophet Muhammad (Salaah alaihi wa salaam) a command "iqrah," meaning to READ?!?

Illiterate means ignorant, according to the Supreme Wisdom, so when I speak on what I call the "Agents of Ignorance" I'm talking about those of you who dislike reading, fall short in your inclination to study, and as a result the rest of us who do study have to waste valuable time and energy contending with those who do not. And this chaotic

---

[1] Supreme Wisdom, Question and Answer No. 7

cycle continues, as I stated in my previous e-mail, with the same people in leadership positions trying to teach and do the same things that they have not been able to successfully teach others to do, manifesting a serious organizationally crippling lack of comprehensive knowledge and wisdom, and we expect different results from said persons? That is indeed insanity! The approaching new year of 2012, for me, represents year number 35 of the metaphorical continuous wandering of the Children of Israel (NOI), meaning only five more years or less to go before the old-minded obstinate and functional illiterates die off, fade away, or what have you and the biblical "Joshuas" and "Calebs" can then stand up and advance on the Promised Land (and not the rented properties) with the militarily trained to develop our beloved Nation of Islam beyond a church. Many of our issues would be resolved in a shorter period of time if we would but read. May Allah bless us all with the charitable spirit and means to give of our time, talent, and what few monetary resources we can spare to make the Salaam restaurant, acquisition of farmland and any other projects successful that enable us to provide food, shelter and clothing to our people.

Your brother,
Harder on the Devil than a thousand ignorant worshipers,
Mikaeel D. S. Muhammad

Jan. 1, 2012

"I'm never concerned with what you know or what you think you know. I will show you what you don't know and what you didn't think about. And that's the way I fight."
- Shihan Mikaeel

"Someone once said that knowledge is power, but he told only a half truth, for knowledge is only potential power. It may become a power only when it is organized and expressed in terms of definite action.

There is a big difference between having an abundance of knowledge and being educated. The difference will become apparent if you look up the Latin root from which the word educate is derived. The word educate comes from the Latin word educare, which means to draw out, to develop from within, to grow through use. It does not mean to acquire and store knowledge!

...success is the power to get whatever one desires in life, without violating the rights of others. Observe that I used the word power! Knowledge is not power but the appropriation and use of other men's knowledge and experience, for the attainment of some definite purpose, is power, moreover, it is power of the most beneficial order."
- Andrew Carnegie

As Salaam Alaikum,

May Allah bless you all with a prosperous year, your steps towards prosperity in the year begins today, take the steps or stand still, move forward or continue wasting time marking time (in drill and in life). Just as I state in my training mantra that every day you don't train is a day you lose an opportunity to gain an advantage over your opposition and mastery over yourself, so it is with success. Every day that you waste in not fulfilling a part of your plan towards achieving your goals and putting off tomorrow what could be done today is a day you have lost and fall short of attaining success. Tomorrow is 365 and a quarter days away and counting down, then it becomes a new year.

Study. Train. Prepare. Work. Grow. Improve. Succeed. Be grateful. Be ever mindful and give thanks to Allah. Help others as we ask Allah to help us. And help God's man in our midst, the Honorable Louis Farrakhan. Peace.

Your brother,
Harder on the Devil than a thousand ignorant worshipers,
Mikaeel D. S. Muhammad

Jan. 2, 2012

"No man's education ever is finished. The man whose Definite Major Purpose in life is of noteworthy proportions must continue to be a student, and he must learn from every possible source - especially those sources from which he can gather specialized knowledge and experience related to his major purpose.

...The successful man makes it his business to read books, and to learn important facts concerning his chosen work which have come from the experience of other men who have gone before him.

A man's reading program should be as carefully chosen as his daily diet, for it, too, is food without which he cannot grow mentally. The man who spends all his reading time on the funny papers and the sex magazines is not headed toward great achievement. A man should include in his daily reading program some material which definitely provides him with knowledge which he can use in the attainment of his major purpose. Random reading may be pleasing, but it seldom is helpful in connection with a man's occupation." - Andrew Carnegie

As-salaam alaikum,

The first revelation to Prophet Muhammad (SAWS) was the command "Read! (Iqrah)." The Honorable Louis Farrakhan read a statistic not long ago that about 51 percent of citizens in this country are functionally illiterate. I tend to think members of the Nation of Islam are not excluded from that statistic, which is why I believe many have not gravitated towards Dianetics (which requires reading and clearing words) or anything else the Hon. Louis Farrakhan has prescribed. Remember the recommended list of books our Leader gave us at the end of Savior's Day 2007 in Detroit? I have yet to meet anyone who has started or completed all of those books. We must become more studious and just as we should be mindful of what we eat, Mr. Carnegie's words ring true of our reading. Strive hard against ignorance, illiteracy, and improper eating. Tomorrow is now less than 364 days away and counting down, if you keep waiting to start tomorrow it will be a new, and another, year gone by (if your diet and daily habits permit you to make it). Respectfully submitted.

Your brother,
Harder on the Devil than a thousand ignorant worshipers,
Mikaeel D. S. Muhammad

Jan. 3, 2012

As salaam alaikum,
For those who may not have attended or heard the 2007 Savior's Day address by the Honorable Louis Farrakhan wherein he stated he wanted us to become readers and also gave a list of materials he wanted us to read, the following is the excerpt from the end of that address:

*"I want you all to get busy and join these ministries and make them work. I want you to become readers. I want you to read **'Without Sanctuary'** by James Allen. I want you to read **'By Way of Deception'** by Victor Ostrovsky. I want you to read **'One Hundred Years of Lynching'** by J.A. Rogers, **'100 Amazing Facts About the Negro'** by J.A. Rogers...**'From Man to Superman'** by J.A. Rogers. I want you to read **'Confessions of an Economic Hitman'** by John Perkins. I want you to read **'Palestine: Peace Not Apartheid'** by Jimmy Carter...former President Jimmy Carter. I want you to read the writings of John Henrik Clark, Cheik Ante Diop, The Most Honorable Elijah Muhammad. I want you to **read 'Hegemony or Survival: America's Quest for Global Dominance'** by Noam Chomsky. I want you to read **'The Secrets of the Federal Reserve'** by Eustice Mullins. I want you to **read 'The Secret Relationship Between Blacks and Jews'**, the Historical Research Department of the Nation of Islam."*

Peace.

Your brother,
Harder on the Devil than a thousand ignorant worshipers,
Mikaeel D. S. Muhammad

Jan. 4, 2012

As salaam alaikum,

In an email correspondence between myself and bro. Anthony (of Atlanta) he sent me an interesting link and quote from bro. Wakeel Allah's (of the Allah Team) Facebook page. From what brother sent me I noted how interesting it was that the rebuilding of the Nation of Islam began with the Hon. Louis Farrakhan being given a book (by bro. Min. Jabril Muhammad). Also, bro. Min. Abdul Allah Muhammad was directed to a book in the Catholic bible (again by bro. Min. Jabril) after a discussion with the Hon. Louis Farrakhan and bro. Min. Jabril. What would have happened if the Hon. Louis Farrakhan refused to read the book given to him that, after reading he stated, caused the scales to be removed from his eyes causing him to comment to bro. Jabril that "the operation was a success"? Many more questions I could ask but I will simply direct this towards the topic of some statements by the late Andrew Carnegie on 'Applied Faith' c. 1908[2]:

"Supreme self-confidence is based upon Faith in Infinite Intelligence, and you may be certain that no one ever attains this state of mind without having a definite belief in Infinite Intelligence and establishing contact with it.

The starting point in the development of self-confidence is Definiteness of Purpose... It is a well-known fact that a man who knows exactly what he wants, has a definite plan for getting it, and is actually engaged in carrying out that plan, has no difficulty in believing in his own ability to succeed. It is equally well-known that the man of indecision, the fellow who flounders around and procrastinates, soon loses confidence in his own ability and winds up doing nothing.

...The power of the mind is so great that it has no limitations other than those which individuals set up in their own minds. The power that removes all limitations from the mind is Faith.

...Faith is developed through deeds. Remember the fact that action must follow the adoption of a definite purpose. Without action, plans and aims are fruitless.

...Faith has sound legs to stand upon when it is backed by definite plans.

...Faith may be developed by clearing the mind of its enemies. Clear the mind of negative thoughts and fears and self-imposed limitations and lo! Faith has filled the place without effort.

...Stop talking about faith and start practicing it.

...We preach sermons and offer up prayers in the name of Christ, yet we rarely make more than a gesture at following His admonition for us to liquidate our problems through the simple state of mind known as Faith. We build great edifices of worship in

---

[2] *'Think Your Way To Wealth'* by Napoleon Hill, pgs 93-114

the name of Christ, yet we profane them with minds that are steeped in fear and self-imposed limitations which He clearly promised us we need not endure.

...mankind needs the quickening influence of plain speech to shock people into recognizing that everything they need or want is already within their grasp. All they need is to take possession of their own minds and use them! To do this, man has no one to consult except himself. The approach to liberty, freedom and abundance of the material necessities and luxuries of life is through the individual's mind. This mind is the only thing over which he has complete control, yet it is the one thing he so seldom uses intelligently.

...self-reliance and Faith are based on definiteness of purpose, back by definite plans of action! Procrastination and Faith have nothing in common.

...The development of Faith is largely a matter of understanding the astounding power of the mind. The only real mystery about Faith is man's failure to make use of it! I speak from personal experience when I say that Faith is a state of mind which can be acquired and used as effectively and easily as any other state of mind. It is all a matter of understanding and application. Truly, "Faith without works is dead."

...Faith is no patented right of mind! It is a universal power as available to the humblest person as it is to the greatest."

And with all of that I say, and with a humble request along with a reminder as the *Holy Qur'an* tells me to say in Surah 49:17, *"Lay me not under an obligation by your Islam; rather Allah lays you under an obligation by guiding you to the faith, if you are truthful."* As I have defined my definite purpose, no one can limit me to what I'm supposed to do or be doing by the confinements and self-imposed limitations of their minds and subconscious fears. Allow no one to do the same to you. "Tomorrow" is less than 361 days away before it is a new year, are you working daily towards achieving your definite purpose or will you sit and wait, like most, for the Hon. Louis Farrakhan (or anyone else) to tell you what you know needs to be done? The Hon. Louis Farrakhan is, and has been, doing what he is supposed to do. The God is waiting on us, Iblis has been respited only until the day we are raised. Let's stop waiting on a Mystery God. Peace.

Your brother,
Harder on the Devil than a thousand ignorant worshipers,
Mikaeel D. S. Muhammad

Jan. 6, 2012

As salaam alaikum,

Andrew Carnegie said the following while being interviewed by Napoleon Hill[3]:

"...the word "educate" means something entirely different from that which many believe it to mean. An educated man is one who has taken possession of his own mind and has so developed it, through organized thought, that it aids him efficiently in the solution of his daily problems in the business of living.

Some people believe that education consists of the acquisition of knowledge, but in a truer sense it means that one has learned how to use knowledge.

I know many men who are walking encyclopedias of knowledge but make such poor use of it they cannot earn a living.

Another mistake that many people make is that of believing that schooling and education are synonymous terms. Schooling may enable a man to acquire knowledge and assemble many useful facts, but schooling alone does not necessarily make a man educated. Education is self-acquired, and it comes through development and use of the mind, and in no other way."

The above describes a "thinking man" as the Hon. Louis Farrakhan expressed that we are to be made into in *'The Meaning of F.O.I.'* It also describes a self-determined individual as well (which is also a 'Clear' in Dianetics). As I quoted the Holy Qur'an Surah 49:17 before, it seems there are a few people who would still like to attempt to lay on me, and others, their "Islam." Well, I won't continue to entertain that, I will simply ask a few (or more)questions. Is this year the year for the continuance of the poor plans and poor execution of said plans made last year that gained little? Are we still making what I will dub the "if the believers just do/give this or that" plans? You know, these are the folks who come before the believers with so-called plans that begin with "if the believers just buy 'x' amount of bean pies/fish dinners then we would have such-and such." Or, "if the believer's (who may already be poor, unemployed, and struggling and sacrificing much as is) give this-or-that we will have..." and then turn around and blame and berate the believers when their plan fails or their business fails. When your plans begin with "if" you are indicating a lack of organizational stability (and ability to strategically plan), and organizational stability is the base of any solid plan of any group (individual and family included).

When I was in the military no 5-paragraph order or briefing for any mission ever began with a commander starting his sentences off with "<u>IF</u> the enemy...", or "<u>IF</u> you Marines..." This type of language, however, I do recall from elementary school fund-raisers back in the 70's where a fundraiser representative would speak before an audience of school children saying "IF" they sold so many boxes of candy they would be able to earn cheap prizes from a cheap list of trinkets that were nowhere near worth the money earned from the students' sales. But even in this it involved door-to-door sales.

---

[3] Ibid., pg 134

And that is about where we are, functioning on an elementary level which is probably another reason why the enemy stated they have us "all but like a church." Or perhaps the short flickers of success from endeavors lull some to sleep and then they awake a few months later realizing an inability to sustain efforts for protracted periods, attempting again to rally others to a cause which yields only a near gain, repeating the same cycle year after year. Short-term solutions never solve long-term problems. And the "if" is always a factor when a leader doesn't know their troops or their troops' capabilities, nor their opposition.

What "IF" they don't do/give this or that, what plan is there then? Are successful businesses and enterprises based on the above type plan? If you currently have a business, has your business been successful with such a plan? Since such plans have not been successful over any protracted period of time, is it insanity to continue carrying out the same type of plan and expecting a different result? Again, organizational stability is key to implementing plans. The right type of leadership is next, with the right kind of definiteness of purpose. Are you the right type of leader? Do you have a clue as to what qualities, traits, and characteristics make-up such a leader? Or are you blindly wandering on in your inordinacy (followed by the blind)?

Rhetorical questions of course, I will post the 31 points Andrew Carnegie stated to Napoleon Hill make up the traits and characteristics of a successful leader. I learned something from it about myself and others, perhaps you will too and be able to share this with others (after applying it to yourself). You are going to see much of Master Fard, the Most Hon. Elijah Muhammad, and the Hon. Louis Farrakhan's teachings in it. Thank you for reading, and there are less than 359 days until tomorrow becomes a new year and the cycle begins again. Procrastination is a self-inflicted wound that proves fatal to individual achievement and success. Use your knowledge/education to benefit self and family. We have been given much by the Creator and work is required to achieve your goals (if you have a clearly defined purpose). Peace.

Your brother,
Harder on the Devil than a thousand ignorant worshipers,
Mikaeel D. S. Muhammad

Chapter 2

So You're In Charge And You Think You're A Leader?
(Parts 1-6)

Jan. 7, 2012

As salaam alaikum,

Military training produces leaders, this has been tried, tested and proven in battles where the loss of lives is the ultimate penalty for leadership errors. Although, everyone who has had military training isn't necessarily a leader, nor did they occupy leadership positions as character is a big part of that. Whether said individuals took advantage of the leadership training that was made available or not, nevertheless, it was available. In 1908, Andrew Carnegie gave Napoleon Hill 31 traits that he stated successful leaders exemplify. When asked by Napoleon Hill, after sharing this list, if all men are capable of becoming successful leaders Andrew Carnegie replied[4], *"Not by any means! You would be surprised to know how few men there are who aspire to become leaders. Most men do not wish to assume the responsibilities of leadership. Others lack the ambition to put forth the extra effort that must go into successful leadership."*

I bear witness to this from my military experience as a noncommissioned officer (NCO), and I also add that being put in charge or telling others you are in charge doesn't make or qualify you as a leader. With that I present *Andrew Carnegie's catalogue of traits exemplified by successful leaders*:

1. The adoption of a Definite Major Purpose and a definite plan for attaining it.

2. The choice of a motive adequate to inspire continuous action in pursuit of the object of one's major purpose. Nothing great is ever achieved without a definite motive.

3. A Master Mind alliance through which to acquire the necessary power for noteworthy achievement. That which one man can accomplish by his own efforts is negligible, confined in the main to the acquisition of the bare necessities of life. Great achievements always is the result of co-ordination of minds working toward a definite end.

4. Self-reliance in proportion to the nature and scope of one's major purpose. No one can go very far without relying largely upon his own efforts, his own initiative, his own judgment.

5. Self-discipline sufficient to give one mastery over both the head and the heart. The man who cannot or will not control himself never can control others. There are no exceptions to this rule. This is so important that it should probably have headed the entire list of the essentials of leadership.

6. Persistence, based on a will to win. Most men are good starters but poor finishers. The man who gives up at the first signs of opposition never goes very far in any undertaking.

---

[4] Ibid., pgs 156-161

7. A well-developed faculty of imagination. Able leaders must be eternally seeking new and better ways of doing things. They must be on the lookout for new ideas and new opportunities to attain the object of their labor. The man who trails along in the old path, doing things merely because others have done them, without looking for methods of improvements, never becomes a great leader.

8. The habit of making definite and prompt decisions at all times. The man who cannot or will not make up his own mind has little opportunity to induce others to follow him.

9. The habit of basing opinions on known facts instead of relying upon guesswork or hearsay evidence. They make it their business to get at the facts before forming judgments, but they move promptly and definitely.

10. The capacity to generate enthusiasm at will and direct it to a definite end. Uncontrolled enthusiasm may be as detrimental as no enthusiasm. Moreover, enthusiasm is contagious, as is also lack of enthusiasm. Followers and subordinates take on the enthusiasm of their leader.

11. A keen sense of fairness and justice under all circumstances. The habit of "playing favorites" is destructive leadership. Men respond best to those who deal with them justly, and especially where they are dealt with fairly by men in higher positions of authority.

12. Tolerance (an open mind) on all subjects at all times. The man with a closed mind does not inspire the confidence of his associates. Without confidence great leadership is an impossibility.

13. The habit of Going The Extra Mile - (doing more than one is paid for and doing it with a positive, agreeable "mental attitude.") This habit on the part of a leader inspires unselfishness on the part of his followers or subordinates. I have never known an able leader in business or industry who did not endeavor at all times to render more service than any man under his authority.

14. Tactfulness and a keen sense of diplomacy, both in spirit and in deed. In a free democracy such as ours, men do not take kindly to brusqueness in their relationships with others.

15. The habit of listening much and talking little. Most people talk too much and say too little. The leader who knows his business knows the value of hearing other men's views. Perhaps we are equipped with two ears, two eyes and only one tongue that we may hear and see twice as much as we speak.

16. An observing nature. The habit of noting small details. All business is a composite of details. The man who does not become familiar with all the details of the work for which he and his subordinates are responsible will not be a successful leader. Moreover, a knowledge of small details is essential for promotion.

17. *Determination. Recognition of the fact that temporary defeat need not be accepted as permanent failure. All men occasionally meet with defeat, in one form or another. The successful leader learns from defeat but he never uses it as an excuse for not trying again. The ability to accept and carry responsibilities is among the more profitable of accomplishments. It is the major need of all industry and business. It pays higher dividends when one assumes responsibility without being required to do so.*

18. *The capacity to stand criticism without resentment. The man who "flares" up with resentment when his work is criticized will never become a successful leader. Real leaders can "take it" and they make it their business to do so. Bigness overlooks the smallness of criticism and carries on.*

19. *Temperance in eating, drinking, and all social habits. The man who has no control over his appetites will have very little control over other people.*

20. *Loyalty to all to whom loyalty is due. Loyalty begins with loyalty to one's self. It extends to one's associates in business. Disloyalty breeds contempt. No one can succeed who "bites the hand that feeds him."*

21. *Frankness with those who have a right to it. Subterfuge which misleads is a poor crutch to lean upon, and it is one that able leaders do not use.*

22. *Familiarity with the nine basic motives which actuate men. (...Emotion of love, emotion of sex, desire for financial gain, desire for self-preservation, desire for freedom of body and mind, desire for self-expression, desire for perpetuation of life after death, emotion of anger, and emotion of fear.) The man who does not understand the natural motives to which men respond will not be a successful leader.*

23. *Sufficient attractiveness of personality to induce voluntary co-operation from others. Sound leadership is based upon effective salesmanship, the ability to be sympathetic and to make one's self pleasing to others.*

24. *The capacity to concentrate full attention on one subject at a time. The jack of all trades is seldom good at any. Concentrated effort gives one power that can be attained in no other way.*

25. *The habit of learning from mistakes - one's own and the mistakes of others.*

26. *Willingness to accept the full responsibility of the mistakes of one's subordinates without trying to "pass the buck." Nothing destroys ones capacity of leadership quicker than the habit of shifting responsibilities to others.*

27. *The habit of adequately recognizing the merits of others, especially when they have done exceptionally good work. Men will often work harder for friendly recognition of their merits than they will for money alone. The successful leader goes out of his way to give credit to his subordinates. A pat on the back denotes confidence.*

28. The habit of applying the Golden Rule principle in all human relationships. The Sermon On the Mount remains a classic for all time, as a sound rule of human relationship. It inspires co-operation that can be had in no other way.

29. A positive "mental attitude" at all times. No one likes a "grouchy," skeptical person who seems to be at outs with the world in general. Such a man will never become an able leader.

30. The habit of assuming full responsibility for each and every task one undertakes, regardless of who actually does the work. Perhaps this quality of leadership should have headed the entire list, and it would have if the qualities of successful leadership had been listed in the order of importance.

31. A keen sense of values. The ability to evaluate in the light of sound judgment without being guided by emotional factors. The habit of putting first things first.

After stating the above Andrew Carnegie (replying to another statement Napoleon Hill made) said:
"Leadership is not entirely a question of the proper mental attitude, although that is an important factor. The successful leader must possess definite knowledge of his life's purpose and work. Men do not like to follow a leader who obviously knows less about his job than they do[5]."

Is it any wonder why we still do not have one military mosque? Professing to be a follower of the Hon. Louis Farrakhan alone does not qualify one for leadership, it might be a pre-requisite but it most certainly doesn't make one qualified. It just won't cut it today. But Praise be to Allah, we have about five more years to fulfill the 40 year biblical time-frame of the Children of Israel (1977-2017) and the old-minded, fearful, rebellious leadership dies off and the "Joshuas" can stand up and seize the initiative on gaining the Promised Land. This is part of the reason I have been counting down the days until the next year and now we have less than 358 days (or 51 weeks) before the new year.

Are you finding it hard to stick to your so-called new year's resolutions? Have you found yourself repeating or falling back into unproductive cycles from last year? Guess what? It doesn't get easier, for just as the Holy Qur'an states that had it been a near gain and a short journey that all would have gone along, the same goes for change and success, neither are near gains or short journeys to attain. Lead, follow, or get the hell out of the way. Still think you are in charge? If you believe so, then you should be found taking responsibility ensuring the welfare of those who you believe you have charge over. This means you are responsible for ensuring they have, or have access to, the basics of food, shelter, clothing, you also see to it they have help resolving personal issues and more. Still think you are a leader as described in the above 31 points? Well, as Surah 49:17 states something to the effect that Allah lays on you an obligation if you are truthful. The masquerades and facades are nothing but falsehood, and falsehood is an ever-vanishing thing, as the Holy Qur'an states. Peace.

---

[5] Ibid., pgs 160-161

Jan. 8, 2012

As salaam alaikum,

  After Andrew Carnegie gave Napoleon Hill the 31 traits essential to a successful leader, in a later interview, Napoleon Hill asked Mr. Carnegie to name the outstanding CAUSES of FAILURE. Mr. Carnegie replied[6] that, "...*it is essential that a practical philosophy of individual achievement include both the causes of success and the causes of failure. You may be surprised to learn that there are more than twice as many major causes of failure as there are causes of success.*" He then listed the following CAUSES of FAILURE:

1. The habit of drifting through life, without a Definite Major Purpose. This is one of the key-causes of failure in that it leads to other causes of failure.

2. Unfavorable physical hereditary foundation at birth. Incidentally, this is the only cause of failure that is not subject to elimination, and even this can be bridged, through the principle of the Master Mind.

3. The habit of meddlesome curiosity concerning other people's affairs, through which time and energy are wasted.

4. Inadequate preparation for the work in which one engages, especially inadequate schooling.

5. Lack of self-discipline, generally manifesting itself through excesses in eating, drinking intoxicating beverages, and sex.

6. Indifference toward opportunities for self-advancement.

7. Lack of ambition to aim above mediocrity.

8. Ill health, often due to wrong thinking, improper diet and exercise.

9. Unfavorable environmental influences during early childhood.

10. Lack of persistence in carrying through to a finish that which one starts (due, in the main, to a lack of definite purpose, and self-discipline).

11. The habit of maintaining a negative "mental attitude" in connection with life generally.

12. Lack of control over the emotions, through controlled habits.

13. The desire for something for nothing, usually expressed through gambling and more offensive habits of dishonesty.

---

[6] Ibid., pgs 263-266

14. *Indecision and indefiniteness.*

15. *One or more of the seven basic fears: (1) poverty (2) criticism (3) ill health (4) loss of love (5) old age (6) loss of liberty (7) death.*

16. *Wrong selection of a mate in marriage.*

17. *Over caution in business and occupational relationships.*

18. *Excess tendency toward chance.*

19. *Wrong choice of associates in business or occupational work.*

20. *Wrong choice of a vocation, or total neglect to make a choice.*

21. *Lack of concentration of effort, leading to dissipation of one's time and energies.*

22. *The habit of indiscriminate spending, without a budget control over income and expenditures.*

23. *Failure to budget and use TIME properly.*

24. *Lack of controlled enthusiasm.*

25. *Intolerance - a closed mind based particularly on ignorance or prejudice in connection with religion, politics and economics.*

26. *Failure to co-operate with others in a spirit of harmony.*

27. *Craving for power or wealth not earned based on merit.*

28. *Lack of a spirit of loyalty where loyalty is due.*

29. *Egotism and vanity not under control.*

30. *Exaggerated selfishness.*

31. *The habit of forming opinions and building plans without basing them on known facts.*

32. *Lack of vision and imagination.*

33. *Failure to make "Master Mind" alliance with those whose experience, education and native ability are needed.*

34. *Failure to recognize the existence of, and the means of adapting one's self to the forces of Infinite Intelligence.*

35. Profanity of speech, reflecting, as it does, evidence of an unclean and undisciplined mind, and an inadequate vocabulary.

36. Speaking before thinking. Talking too much.

37. Covetousness, revenge, and greed.

38. The habit of procrastination, often based on plain laziness, but generally the result of lack of a definite major purpose.

39. Speaking slanderously of other people, with or without cause.

40. Ignorance of the nature and purpose of the power of thought, and lack of knowledge of the principles of operation of the mind.

41. Lack of personal initiative, due, in the main, to the lack of a definite major purpose.

42. Lack of self-reliance, due, also, to absence of an obsessional motive founded on a definite major purpose.

43. Lack of qualities of a pleasing personality.

44. Lack of faith in one's self, in the future, in one's fellow men, in God.

45. Failure to develop the power of will, through voluntary, controlled habits of thought.

Andrew Carnegie further stated that:
"These are not all the causes of failure, but they represent the major portion of them. All these causes, except number two, can be eliminated or brought under control, through application of the principle of definiteness of a major purpose and mastery of the will-power. You might say, therefore, that the first and last of these causes of failure control all the others except one."

Analyze the successful leadership traits and the major causes of failure. Are you one of those of the mindset that is still waiting on the Hon. Louis Farrakhan to tell you what you are supposed to do or what your definite major purpose is? Are you telling others that they too must wait because you think that is sound wisdom (when it isn't wisdom at all)? He has already stated he doesn't know what Allah put in each of us so why are you waiting to be told what to do (because you really don't know what to do, how to do, why you should)? What will you do when the Hon. Louis Farrakhan departs and you are depending on him to tell you what you are supposed to do? Guess you will continue to wait on the Mystery god like over 85% of the population does. Is your gut still hanging and protruding out demonstrating a lack of mastery over your diet and that your intestines/colon is full of fecal impacted matter (you are literally full of sh*t)? Are you waiting still until tomorrow to start the steps and discipline towards your definite major purpose, and also representing the Messenger's teaching in deed instead of lip-profession? Tomorrow is now less than 357 days away until the new year. Are you striving to READ, being mindful and careful of what you read just as you are careful of your diet? Or do you see that you have not been careful of your diet and your reading (or lack of interest in reading) is a mental reflection as your diet is a physical reflection? The Messenger gave us the keys and most of us are content with holding onto the keys but never opening any doors to exit the prison of our minds to venture into the Big Fields. Perhaps you are not truly "wide awake" or too lazy, or lack the ambition. Or perhaps you are and have been a victim of or guilty of the above listed major causes of failure. So you really think you are in charge and you call yourself a leader?? Yes, you just may be in charge and this may be why those who follow you are not realizing their definite major purpose and experiencing success, and why you are not successful because you have no true understanding of what successful leadership entails. Suppressive Personalities seem to gravitate toward leadership positions according to the Dianetics teachings on Ethics. And the Suppressive Personalities (SP's) are always surrounded by Potential Trouble Sources (PTT's). Don't allow anyone to suppress the talents Allah has blessed you with. Wake up and discover the Big Fields awaiting you! May Allah bless the believers with success who exercise, emulate and cultivate daily the habits of success!

Your brother,
Harder on the Devil than a thousand ignorant worshipers,
Mikaeel D. S. Muhammad

Jan. 11, 2012

As Salaam Alaikum,
The Holy Qur'an reminds us that with difficulty comes ease. The **Holy Qur'an** also outlines the pretexts for its guidance in **Surah 2:2-5:**

2) This Book, there is no doubt in it, is a guide to those who keep their duty,
3) Who believe in the Unseen and keep up prayer and spend out of what We have given them,
4) And who believe in that which has been revealed to thee and that which was revealed before thee, and of the Hereafter they are sure.
5) These are on a right course from their Lord and these it is that are successful.

Now, verse (ayat) 2:2 is really significant, again, as it reveals that the Holy Qur'an is a guide to "those who keep their duty." Duty is another expression for "Definiteness of Purpose." Self- determination is a pre-requisite for definiteness of purpose and if you have not yet become a thinking man, as the Hon. Louis Farrakhan stated we are to be made into in the *'Meaning of F.O.I.'*, and someone else is defining your purpose for you then you have not yet become self-determined. The purpose of auditing in Dianetics is to free you from painful engrams (rooted in fear, as fear can be associated with pain) to produce a 'Clear', which is a self-determined person. If you have not yet become self-determined then you cannot honestly say that you are keeping your duty. How can you expect guidance from the Holy Qur'an, or any other book, if you don't know what your definiteness of purpose/duty is? And so books will provide no guidance to the person who has no definiteness of purpose, so how effective is selling the *Final Call Newspaper* to 51% of the population who are functionally illiterate without helping our people understand how to overcome illiteracy, what their purpose in life is or how to become self-determined and fulfill their definiteness of purpose? Our struggle in going after our people is what to do with them once we get them. Well if you, as a leader, are waiting on the Hon. Louis Farrakhan to tell you what your purpose is and what needs to be done because you honestly don't know what you are supposed to do, how to do it, why you should, and fail at overcoming the obstacles in your path, how can you give direction and guidance to those you go after? The FCN is a tool, and like any other tool it is useless if it is not taught or known how the tool is to be used and for what purpose. And if you don't read as a daily habit, or you are of the functionally illiterate, you can't possibly motivate others or teach others to do successfully what you are not successfully doing.

We are definitely in troubled times and we all are facing difficulties and adversity. The ease that comes with the difficulties that the Holy Qur'an speaks about can be understood from another perspective given by Napoleon Hill who stated:

"Every adversity carries with it the seed of an equivalent benefit!...The "seed of an equivalent benefit" that is to be found in every adversity consists of the opportunity one has to use the experience as a means of developing his willpower, by accepting it as a mental stimulant to greater action."

'Organizing for Success' is the title of a course I successfully completed from Dianetics/Scientology Org. last year which was recommended to me by bro. Jon Muhammad (who also completed it) from Los Angeles at Savior's Day 2011. The interesting thing about this workbook course is that the language and material for organizing is nearly identical to what I was exposed to in the military and when I remarked about this was when I was told by members at the Scientology Org that L.R. Hubbard was a veteran officer of the U.S. Navy. I stated before that organizational stability is the foundation of any successful plan and often times we have been told what needs to be done but not how to do it and so those who are in leadership positions drift continuously trying to lead others and direct others into the "how to's" according to what they believe should be done, whether they are productive/beneficial in the long run or not. I'm sure the leaders of the biblical Children of Israel did the same things, drifting and wandering outside of the Promised Land, afraid to challenge the obstacles there and believing they were doing the right thing.

Ferdinand F. Fournies stated that *"One of life's truths is that if you believe the wrong things, you will do wrong things on purpose and, conversely, if you believe the right things, you will do right things on purpose....merely believing the right things is not enough; you must do the right things to be successful."* The old-minded were not successful in entering and taking over the Promised Land and none were permitted to so they wandered and drifted until they died off. Joshua and his followers did what they were supposed to and were granted success.

We are constantly told what we should do (or you may be telling others what they should do) but not how to do, and if you don't know how to do whatever it is you should be doing then most likely you really don't know or understand the purpose of what you are supposed to do (definiteness of purpose) which means you will likely fail at it. Remember, Islam comes after all else fails. And why would all else fail? Because without definiteness of purpose "all else" is not in line with the steps of success and God's Will. And Islam represents submission to Allah's Will which has been hardwired into each of our DNA, which is why we are Muslim by nature.

Lastly, Napoleon Hill claimed to have had an interview with the Devil in Washington D.C., 1938, which he outlined in his manuscript entitled *'Outwitting the Devil'* just after his publication *'Think And Grow Rich.'* Now whether this "interview" was a figment of his imagination, a conversation with himself, or a conversation with another Caucasian is of no significance to me, however, the "Devil's" responses to his questions is significant. In particular, his answers on the subject of what they call 'drifting/drifters,' which the Devil claims to have control over as he says *"I cause people to allow me to do their thinking for them because they are too lazy and too indifferent to think for themselves."* When Napoleon Hill asks "the Devil" to describe a typical drifter the following extensive answer is given[7]:

"The first thing you will notice about a drifter is his total lack of a major purpose in life.

---

[7] Pages 91-93, 'Outwitting the Devil', Napoleon Hill

24

He will be conspicuous by his lack of self-confidence.

He will never accomplish anything requiring thought and effort.

He spends all he earns and more too, if he can get credit.

He will be sick or ailing from some real or imaginary cause, and calling to high heaven if he suffers the least physical pain.

He will have little or no imagination.

He will lack enthusiasm and initiative to begin anything he is not forced to undertake, and he will plainly express his weakness by taking the line of least resistance whenever he can do so.

He will be ill-tempered and lacking in control over his emotions.

His personality will be without magnetism and it will not attract people.

He will have opinions on everything but accurate knowledge of nothing.

He may be jack of all trades but good at none.

He will neglect to cooperate with those around him, even those on whom he must depend for food and shelter.

He will make the same mistake over and over again, never profiting by failure.

He will be narrow-minded and intolerant on all subjects, ready to crucify those who may disagree with him.

He will expect everything of others but be willing to give little or nothing in return.

He may begin things but complete nothing.

He will be loud in his condemnation of his government, but he will never tell you definitely how it can be improved.

He will never reach decisions on anything if he can avoid it, and if he is forced to decide he will reverse himself at the first opportunity.

He will eat too much and exercise too little.

He will take a drink of liquor if someone else pays for it.

He will gamble if he can do it "on the cuff."

He will criticize others who are succeeding in their chosen calling. In brief, the drifter will work harder to get out of thinking than most others work in earning a good living.

He will tell a lie rather than admit his ignorance on any subject.

If he works for other, he will criticize them to their backs and flatter them to their faces."

Now, I will site the non-drifter in the next message, but I also add that this "Devil" sited that the three persons who unknowingly serve his purpose in gaining control over children's minds were parents, schoolteachers, and religious instructors. Remember in the Holy Qur'an that Iblis states he would come at them from before them and after them, the left and right, and even in their straight path. More coming, insha-Allah.

Your brother,
Harder on the Devil than a thousand ignorant worshipers,
Mikaeel D. S. Muhammad

Jan. 12, 2012

As salaam alaikum,

   Continuing with Napoleons Hill's alleged interview in 1938 with "the Devil," according to this Devil there were three people unknowingly manipulated to carry out his work of controlling 98% of the population, getting them when they are children, these three people were parents, school teachers, and religious instructors (Remember Iblis' words in the Holy Qur'an of coming at us from all directions, even in our straight path). Here's how he claims to use each in the following answers given:

"One of my favorite tricks is to coordinate the efforts of parents and religious instructors so they work together in helping me to destroy the children's power to think for themselves. I use many religious instructors to undermine the courage and power of independent thought of children, by teaching them to fear me; but I use parents to aid the religious leaders in this great work of mine...I accomplish this through a very clever trick. I cause the parents to teach their children to believe as the parents in connection with religion, politics, marriage, and other important subjects. In this way, as you can see, when I gain control of the mind of a person I can easily perpetuate the control by causing that person to help me fasten it upon the minds of his offspring...
I cause children to become drifters by following the example of their parents, most of whom I have already taken over and bound eternally to my cause. In some parts of the world I gain mastery over children's minds and subdue their will power in exactly the same way that men break and subdue animals of lower intelligence. It makes no difference to me how a child's will is subdued, as long as it fears something. I will enter its mind through that fear and limit the child's power to think independently...
Accurate thought is death to me. I cannot exist in the minds of those who think accurately. I do not mind people thinking as long as they think in terms of fear, discouragement, hopelessness, and destructiveness. When they begin to think in constructive terms of faith, courage, hope, and definiteness of purpose, they immediately become allies of my opposition and therefore lost to me.

Schoolteachers help me gain control of the minds of children not so much by what they teach the children as because of what they do not teach them. The entire public school system is so administered that it helps my cause by teaching children almost everything except how to use their own minds and think independently. I live in fear that someday some courageous person will reverse the present system of school teaching and deal my cause a death blow by allowing the students to become the instructors, using those who serve as teachers only as guides to help the children establish ways and means of developing their own minds from within...School children are taught not to develop and use their own minds, but to adopt and use the thoughts of others. This sort of schooling destroys the capacity for independent thought, except in a few rare cases where children rely so definitely upon their own will power that they refuse to allow others to do their thinking.[8]"

---

[8] 'Outwitting The Devil', N. Hill, pgs 79-82

There is so much more to this book *'Outwitting the Devil'*, and significant that it was written in 1938, but I will lastly site the summary given on this subject and then as I listed the description of the drifter I will cite the non-drifter.

Napoleon Hill's Devil continues:
"I cause it to appear that everything done by the parents, the schoolteachers, and the religious instructors is being done by my opposition.

This diverts attention from me while I manipulate the minds of the young. When religious instructors try to teach children the virtues of my opposition, they generally do so by frightening them with my name. That is all I ask of them. I kindle the flame of fear into proportions which destroy the child's power to think accurately. In the public schools the teachers further my cause by keeping the children so busy cramming non-essential information into their minds they have no opportunity to think accurately or to analyze correctly the things their instructors teach them[9]."

The "drifter" was described as *"Those who do little or no thinking for themselves... A drifter is one who permits himself to be influenced and controlled by circumstances outside of his own mind."* I believe this also describes the Dianetics "Reactive Mind" which is how the majority of people respond to situations and things we read (without 'Clearing' words) and life in general, using the Reactive Mind whether we realize it or not, hence the need for Auditing to tap into use of the Analytical Mind producing accurate thought. And now for the description of characteristics of the 'non-drifter'[10]:

"The first sign of a non-drifter is this: He is always engaged in doing something definite, through some well-organized plan which is definite. He has a major goal in life toward which he is always working, and many minor goals, all of which lead toward his central scheme.

The tone of his voice, the quickness of his step, the sparkle in his eyes, the quickness of his decisions clearly mark him as a person who knows exactly what he wants and is determined to get it, no matter how long it may take or what price he must pay.

If you ask him questions, he gives direct answers and never falls back on evasions or resorts to subterfuge.

He extends many favors to others, but accepts favors sparingly or not at all.

He will be found up front whether he is playing a game or fighting a war.

If he does not know the answers he will say so frankly.

He has a good memory; never offers an alibi for his shortcomings. He never blames others for his mistakes no matter if they deserve the blame.

---

[9] Ibid., pg 83
[10] Ibid., pgs 93-94

He used to be known as a go-getter, but in modern times he is called a go-giver. You will find him running the biggest business in town, living on the best street, driving the best automobile, and making his presence felt wherever he happens to be.

He is an inspiration to all who come into contact with his mind.

The major distinguishing feature of the non-drifter is this: He has a mind of his own and uses it for all purposes."

Thank you for reading, to be continued, insha'-Allah.

Your brother,
Harder on the Devil than a thousand ignorant worshipers,
Mikaeel D. S. Muhammad

Jan. 13, 2012

As salaam alaikum,

Master Fard Muhammad studied for 42 years, the Most Hon. Elijah Muhammad was taught day and night by him for three years and four months and then continued on his given assignment of study and labored for 44 years. The Hon. Louis Farrakhan studied for hours and hours daily, and labored nearly 20 years by the time the Messenger departed, and then picked up and continued his study and labor about 3 years after the Messenger's departure. The great and influential jazz artist John Coltrane was said to have studied/practiced up to 15 hours a day for 3 years at an early time of his music career. Michael Jordan was up at, and into, the wee hours of the morning and night practicing and improving his game. All of the greats in any endeavor have this similar quality about themselves of going the extra mile in study and practice which propelled them to the forefront of their discipline/art. We, who claim to be followers of the Most Hon. Elijah Muhammad through the guidance of the Hon. Louis Farrakhan, can not make good on that claim unless we are found diligently studying to improve ourselves. Perhaps this a part of the reason why our communities have not been developed and cultivated because we have not understood (after all of this time) our leader's study guides (or guides to study/ing) entitled *'Self-Improvement: The Basis For Community Development.'* As self-improvement is the basis of community development **STUDY IS THE BASIS OF SELF-IMPROVEMENT!** How can we cultivate the leader within if we don't study and we don't have a clue what is within us (mentally and physically)? It may be surprising to most how many adults walk around without a clue as to how their own organs function, what chemicals are produced or broken down by each gland, let alone where exactly each organ is within their own body. We, for the most part are poor students of behavioral psychology, physiology or any other matters of the brain and body. Sadly, just about everything one would want to know about such topics has already been written and illustrated in volumes and volumes of books (and now the internet as well), but we won't read in the name of our Lord. And so, today we are the best fulfillers of the biblical axiom of a people destroyed for a lack of knowledge because we reject knowledge.

Back to the continued topic, as stated before in part 1 of this subject Napoleon Hill was given 31 traits that a successful leader exemplifies. Number 22 was *"Familiarity with the nine basic motives which actuate men."* These nine basic motives are:

1. Emotion of love
2. Emotion of sex
3. Desire for financial gain
4. Desire for self-preservation
5. Desire for freedom of body and mind
6. Desire for self-expression
7. Desire for perpetuation of life after death
8. Emotion of anger, and
9. Emotion of fear.

And it was stated that *"The man who does not understand the natural motives to which men respond will not be a successful leader[11]."* Of the four emotions and five desires listed, the two emotions of anger and fear are the worst motives a leader could try to use to actuate men. Also, 'guilt' is not and has never been a motive which actuates men in any worthy cause. But the leader who attempts to use guilt as a motive is really operating out of the 'Emotion of Fear' whether they realize it or not, and that fear is the fear of failure, either being looked at as a failure or failure in general.

In his book *'Outwitting the Devil,'* Napoleon Hill's Devil states that 'failure' is one of his most effective devices (after "flattery") for causing people to become "drifters." He states the following on 'failure':

"One of my most effective devices is failure! The majority of people begin to drift as soon as they meet with opposition, and not one out of ten thousand will keep on trying after failing two or three times... Failure breaks down one's morale, destroys self-confidence, subdues enthusiasm, dulls imagination, and drives away definiteness of purpose.
  Without these qualities no one can permanently succeed in any undertaking..."

[Whether you recall me explaining/teaching or not, 'Morale' or moral conduct is one of the four characteristics that enable a soldier to overcome fear]

He then states that the *"capacity to surmount failure without being discouraged"* is *"the chief asset of every man who attains outstanding success in any calling.[12]"*

Thank you for reading, more coming insha'-Allah. Also, thanks to those who messaged me saying how the information given has helped them, may Allah continue to bless you with hindsight, insight, and foresight to guide you aright in the path of light. Iqrah! READ in the name of thy Lord...

Your brother,
Harder on the Devil than a thousand ignorant worshipers,
Mikaeel D. S. Muhammad

---

[11] Think Your Way To Wealth, N. Hill, pg 160
[12] Outwitting The Devil, N. Hill, pgs 104-105

Jan. 14, 2012

As salaam alaikum,
Continuing on with Napoleon Hill's alleged interview with "the Devil," the question was asked of what suggested changes could be made to reverse the weakness of the public school system. This lengthy answer would help us tremendously to go after the youth and actually undo the damage done by parents, schoolteachers, and religious instructors that makes the youth rebellious against parents, high-school drop-outs, and rejecters of right guidance through the religion of Islam (or any other right guidance) as represented by the teachings of the Most Hon. Elijah Muhammad and his servant the Hon. Louis Farrakhan. It is said that if we knew better we would do better, and since we seem to fall into and repeat cycles of ineffective and unsuccessful methods of doing things then we have yet to prove we have learned and know better. The answer to Napoleon Hill's question (in 1938 I remind you) was given as follows:

"Reverse the present system by giving children the privilege of leading in their school work instead of following orthodox rules designed only to impart abstract knowledge. Let instructors serve as students and let the students serve as instructors.

As far as possible, organize all school work into definite methods through which the student can learn by doing, and direct the class work so that every student engages in some form of practical labor connected with the daily problems of life.

Ideas are the beginning of all human achievement. Teach all students how to recognize practical ideas that may be of benefit in helping them acquire whatever they demand of life.

Teach the students how to budget and use time, and above all teach the truth that time is the greatest asset available to human beings and the cheapest.

Teach the student the basic motives by which all people are influenced and show how to use these motives in acquiring the necessities and the luxuries of life.

Teach children what to eat, how much to eat, and what is he relationship between proper eating and sound health.

Teach children the true nature and function of the emotion of sex, and above all, teach them that it can be transmuted into a driving force capable of lifting one to great heights of achievement.

Teach children to be definite in all things, beginning with the choice of a definite major purpose in life!

Teach children the nature of and possibilities for good and evil in the principle of habit, using as illustrations with which to dramatize the subject the everyday experiences of children and adults.

Teach children how habits become fixed through the law of hypnotic rhythm, and influence them to adopt, while in the lower grades, habits that will lead to independent thought!

Teach children the difference between temporary defeat and failure, and show them how to search for the seed of an equivalent advantage which comes with every defeat.

Teach children to express their own thoughts fearlessly and accept or reject, at will, all ideas of others, reserving to themselves, always, the privilege of relying upon their own judgment.

Teach children to reach decisions promptly and to charge them, if at all, slowly and with reluctance, and never without a definite reason.

Teach children that the human brain is the instrument with which one receives, from the great storehouses of nature, the energy which is specialized into definite thoughts; that the brain does not think, but serves as an instrument for the interpretation of stimuli which cause thought.

Teach children the value of harmony in their own minds and that this is attainable only through self-control.

Teach children the nature and the value of self-control.

Teach children that there is a law of increasing returns which can be and should be put into operation, as a matter of habit, by rendering always more service and better service than is expected of them.

Teach children the true nature of the Golden Rule, and above all show them that through the operation of this principle, everything they do to and for another they do also to and for themselves.

Teach children not to have opinions unless they are formed from facts or beliefs which may reasonably be accepted as facts.

Teach children that cigarettes, liquor, narcotics, and over-indulgence in sex destroy the power of will and lead to the habit of drifting. Do not forbid these evils - just explain them.

Teach children the danger of believing anything merely because their parents, religious instructors, or someone else says it is so.

Teach children to face facts, whether they are pleasant or unpleasant, without resorting to subterfuge or offering alibis.

Teach children to encourage the use of their sixth sense through which ideas present themselves in their minds from unknown sources, and to examine all such ideas carefully.

Teach children the full import of the law of compensation as it was interpreted by Ralph Waldo Emerson, and show them how the law works in the small, everyday affairs of life.

Teach children that definiteness of purpose, backed by definite plans persistently and continuously applied, is the most efficacious form of prayer available to human beings.

Teach children that the space they occupy in this world is measured definitely by the quality and quantity of useful service they render the world.

Teach children there is no problem which does not have an appropriate solution and that the solution often may be found in the circumstance creating the problem.

Teach children that their only real limitations are those which they set up or permit others to establish in their own minds.

Teach them that man can achieve whatever man can conceive and believe!

Teach children that all schoolhouses and all textbooks are elementary implements which may be helpful in the development of their minds, but that the only school of real value is the great University of Life wherein one has the privilege of learning from experience.

Teach children to be true to themselves at all times and, since they cannot please everybody, therefore to do a good job of pleasing themselves[13]."

As you reflect over these suggestions I remind you that you cannot teach someone to do successfully what you are not successfully doing, therefore in order for us to teach the youth we must first learn and adopt these suggestions ourselves, incorporate and exercise them which will enable us to better improve ourselves. Napoleon Hill was told that the preparation necessary to move with definiteness of purpose was gaining mastery over self and that *"The person who is not master himself can never be master of others."* When he asked *"Where should one begin when making a start at control over self?"* the answer given to him was *"By mastering the three appetites responsible for most of one's lack of self-discipline. The three appetites are (1) the desire for food, (2) the desire for expression of sex, (3) the desire to express loosely organized opinions."* So if you are in charge of anything, or you think you are in charge, but you have not taken charge of yourself and mastered these three appetites then you can not seriously expect to successfully lead others or be respected as a leader by others. Especially by those who not only follow but adhere to the teachings of the Most Hon. Elijah Muhammad and *'How to Eat to Live.'* Eating one meal a day or one meal every

---

[13] Outwitting the Devil, N. Hill, pgs 174-178

34

two or three days (and eating the right foods) as the Most Hon. Elijah Muhammad prescribed for us is the key to mastering the first appetite. NO EXCUSES! Leadership is by example, soldiers (and former Marines) don't respect any other type of leadership, neither does the youth. So you ARE in charge,...of yourself, and if you think you are a leader then lead by example and demonstrate mastery over the three major appetites and you will prove such. Thank you for reading, this concludes this topic. May Allah bless you to master yourself.

Your brother,
Harder on the Devil than a thousand ignorant worshipers,
Mikaeel D. S. Muhammad

Section 2

Military Clearance

"The old military training must be thrown out of the window because that was not a training to save our people. You were often being trained in the manner of the army of the devil. And you never did look upon yourself as an army of Saviours. You looked upon yourself as an army of killers. And that's why if you didn't have no devil in front of you to kill, several of you turned on each other, threatening each other, jumping in each other's chest. That's not the way that Allah wanted us to be militarily trained."

– Hon. Louis Farrakhan, *The Meaning of F.O.I.* (pgs 9-10)

Chapter 3
Military Training Implies War!

"The 47th chapter of the Quran is called, "Muhammad," and that chapter is also called "War" because when the Muhammad of the Holy Quran comes he makes war on the forces of evil that have ruled and dominated the planet earth for the last 6,000 years. The objective of it is to turn the earth back into the hands of its original owners."
        - Hon. Louis Farrakhan, *'Meaning of F.O.I.'* (page 1)

...But the enemy has been wise enough, though he is smaller in number, to go among the Original people and color them and make them agents of the colored man rather than agents of the Original God." – Hon. Louis Farrakhan, *'Meaning of F.O.I.'* (page 2)

Remember, the "Colored Man" does not represent people "of color," though they mistakenly refer to themselves as such. Of course, you will find the word "colored" in modern dictionaries is defined as "non-white skin" when used as an adjective, however the suffix "ed" denotes past-tense of an action, or something already done. The root word *'color'* comes from the old Latin word *'colos'* which originally meant *"a covering,"* akin to the Latin word *'celere'* meaning *"to hide or conceal."* So what was covered, hidden, or concealed in the trick of the former slave-masters of the Original man and woman getting us to refer to ourselves as "Coloreds"? The discovery and use of germ-warfare by Caucasians in the past and present should give you a clue as to what has been, and is being, done to people of color world-wide. By the definition of the "powers that be" we have become "Coloreds" because they hid and concealed the history, knowledge and wisdom of our roots from us and injected us with their perverse Western way of thinking, theology, and philosophy. They have also used germ-warfare, or biological warfare, along with chemical warfare to hide the most bio-disruptive viruses and diseases in vaccinations they administer to people of color (people possessing melanin) globally. This warfare is also used in the foodstuffs and medicines that we consume causing us to be prone to cancer, HIV/AIDS, and other degenerative dis-eases. So we refer to Caucasians as the real "Colored man" because he colors (changes) the thinking and reality of people from the original and what is truth, and once colored, we no longer think or act like our original selves nor do we see what is hidden and concealed in their codes and coded language we use that keeps us in an inferior state of mind and existence.

But what makes one an agent of the Colored Man? *Agent* is defined as "one who acts," from the Latin word *'agentum'* meaning "effective, powerful" and from *'agere'* meaning "to set in motion, drive, lead, conduct." So when one acts, knowingly or unknowingly, and sets in motion, or leads, or conducts himself/herself in such a way as to bring about an effective or powerful change that benefits those in opposition to God's Will, especially to the detriment and death of their own people known as the Original Man and Woman, then that one can be considered an "agent" of the Colored Man. But one can also be an agent working in harmony with God's Will. Then of course there are always the "double-agents" who try to play both sides to benefit themselves, this double-agent could also be described as a hypocrite.

"Whether you know it or not, we are at war! Our survival as a people is at stake and no weak kneed cowardly leaders need to stand in front of Black people today! This is a time for real men! Men that understand that in order for people to be free, sacrifice has to be made, the loss of life has to take place, blood must flow in order for people who are enslaved to be free!" – Hon. Louis Farrakhan, Oct. 9, 2011, *'Holy Day of Atonement'* address, Philadelphia, PA

"War is thus an act of force to compel our enemy to do our will." – Carl Von Clausewitz, *'On War'*

What is the will of the opposers of truth? What is God's Will? The opposition to truth has "forced" us, willingly and unwillingly, knowingly and unknowingly, to do their will. And so God has come, in the Person of Master Fard Muhammad, to force upon us a choice, to do his will or continue doing other than and suffer the consequences. Part of God's Will is for us to accept our own and be ourselves, which he (Master Fard) taught that our self is a righteous Muslim (one who submits to do God's Will).

War Defined

The various techniques used in war is referred to as 'Warfare.' The history of warfare as we know it stems from, and has transitioned from a little over 6,000 years ago when the Caucasian race came into existence through the process of genetic birth control and genetic engineering also known as "grafting," which is accomplished by killing the dominant black germ and sparing the recessive brown germ. This process determined the nature of the by-product of the end of this genetic engineering which is people with blonde hair, blue eyes, and deficient of melanin. For those who don't understand the nature of why the Caucasian must engage in warfare in the manner in which he does, and his motives for such, Dr. Francis Cress-Welsing gives profound insight in her book *'The Isis Papers: Keys to the Colors'*. Their (Caucasian) warfare against people possessing melanin around the world is predicated on her 'Color-Confrontation theory', which is best summarized as fear of white genetic annihilation.

The English word war can be traced etymologically to the Old High German *werran*, and the German *verwirren*, meaning "to confuse," "to perplex," and "to bring into confusion." And Sun Tzu in the *'Art of War,'* long before there was a German language, stated that *"All war is based on deception"* (translated from the ancient Chinese language of course). I stated in the Preface to this volume that every war the United States government has engaged in have all been based on deception, lies.

Former President Dwight Eisenhower (who was also a retired 5-star General) stated in his farewell address in January of 1961:

"...We now stand ten years past the midpoint of a century that has witnessed four major wars among great nations. Three of these involved our own country. Despite these holocausts America is today the strongest, the most influential and most productive nation in the world. Understandably proud of this pre-eminence, we yet realize that America's leadership and prestige depend, not merely upon our unmatched material progress, riches and military strength, but on how we use our power in the interests of world peace and human betterment.

Throughout America's adventure in free government, such basic purposes have been to keep the peace; to foster progress in human achievement, and to enhance liberty, dignity and integrity among peoples and among nations..."

Of course he was not speaking to the masses of peoples of color who were not experiencing these professed basic purposes of peace, progress and enhanced liberty, dignity and integrity from the so-called "Powers that be." Nevertheless, his speech was very profound.

An even more profound writing comes from a well-known Marine Corps General, Major General Smedley D. Butler. Now, to the uninitiated, Maj.Gen. Smedley D. Butler is the most highly decorated and renowned officer in the history of the United States Marine Corps. Knowledge of him is standard information drilled into each and every recruit who goes through Marine Corps Boot-camp. His name is tied to the Marines just as baseball and apple pie are tied to the American past-time. However, what is little known or never discussed is that after serving 33 years in the Marines as a highly decorated, highly respected, and honorable serviceman, he became a staunch anti-war proponent, and very vocal opponent to this country's military actions during the Great Depression and his writings can be found in a book he entitled *'War Is A Racket'* (originally published in 1935). He is also responsible for exposing and bringing down a fascist corporate plot manufactured by several Wall Street bankers, of which he gave testimony before a Congressional Committee in the mid-1930's. I cite the following from his book, chapter 1 page 23:

"War is a racket. It always has been. It is possibly the oldest, easily the most profitable, surely the most vicious. It is the only one international in scope. It is the only one in which the profits are reckoned in dollars and the losses in lives.

A racket is best described, I believe, as something that is not what it seems to the majority of people. Only a small "inside" group knows what it is about. It is conducted for the benefit of the very few, at the expense of the very many. Out of war a few people make huge fortunes.

In the World War a mere handful garnered the profits of the conflict. At least 21,000 new millionaires and billionaires were made in the United States during the World War. That many admitted their huge blood gains in their income tax returns. How many other war millionaires falsified their income tax returns no one knows."

Mind you, he is speaking about World War I (1914-1918). Can you imagine being a millionaire or billionaire in 1918? This is just over a decade before the so-called Great Depression. As the Hon. Louis Farrakhan says in the *'Meaning of F.O.I.'* I want you to become *"thinking men."* On pages 34-35 Maj. Gen. Butler states the following:

"Up to and including the Spanish-American War, we had a prize system, and soldiers and sailors fought for money. During the Civil War they were paid bonuses, in many instances, before they went into service. The government, or states, paid as high as $1,200 for an enlistment. In the Spanish-American War they gave prize money. When we captured any vessels, the soldiers all got their share – at least, they were supposed to. Then it was found that we could reduce the cost of wars by taking all the prize money and keeping it, but conscripting the soldier anyway. Then the soldiers couldn't bargain for their labor. Everyone else could bargain, but the soldier couldn't.

Napoleon once said, "All men are enamored of decorations…they positively hunger for them."

So, by developing the Napoleonic system – the medal business – the government learned it could get soldiers for less money, because the boys like to be decorated. Until the Civil War there were no medals. Then the Congressional Medal of Honor was handed out. It made enlistments easier. After the Civil War no new medals were issued until the Spanish-American War.

In the World War, we used propaganda to make the boys accept conscription. They were made to feel ashamed if they didn't join the army.

So vicious was this war propaganda that even God was brought into it. With few exceptions our clergymen joined in the clamor to kill, kill, kill."

I am going to revisit Maj. Gen. Butler's book in my chapter on "Conscientious Objector." I listed all of the above to illustrate, and hopefully make clear, what war is and why our military training must be rooted in study and is unlike the military training of this world. The majority of our people are walking around as victims of Post-Traumatic Stress Disorder (PTSD) and, for the most part, they have never stepped foot in the "Theater of War" but we all are exposed to and face the elements found in a combat environment daily. We must constantly train and condition ourselves, mentally, physically, and most certainly spiritually, to meet and overcome every obstacle in our path to righteous conduct and growth.

Chapter 4

What Is An NCO and Why Is It Not Mentioned in the Supreme Wisdom?

The General Orders

Over the past 20 years during the men's training class, also known as 'F.O.I. Class', I have heard during the drill portion of the classes "want-to-be" drill instructors question men in ranks about their General Orders. The question would be asked "What is your sixth general order!?," to which most would reply "Sir! My sixth general order is...to receive, obey, and pass on to the sentry who relieves me, all orders from the commanding officer, officer of the day and non-commissioned officers of the guard only!" When I first heard this I thought to myself how close the response sounded to the General Orders I was made to learn in basic training (Boot Camp) in the United States Marine Corps. Very close in deed but with a few words omitted. I have also heard, over the years, brothers ask what a non-commissioned officer is as well. So when one is asked if they "know" their General Orders and has no clue as to what a non-commissioned officer, or NCO is, how can one truly "know" their General Orders? I have explained in volume 1 of this work what a 'commission' is and one could not quite grasp what a 'non-commissioned officer' is unless they knew what constituted a commission (See Volume 1). The Most Hon. Elijah Muhammad taught us to get at the root of a thing to truly understand it and so let me make this as plain as possible as we dig into the root.

Starting with the General Orders that have been adopted by the Fruit of Islam (F.O.I.) of the Nation of Islam, I have oft-repeated that these General Orders come directly from the U.S. Marine Corps and NOT from Master Fard Muhammad or the Messenger as some seem to think and have incorrectly repeated to others such an idea. As I have often stated that 'Military' has its own language, if one were not familiar with said language and thoroughly versed in it then when that language is adopted from the military and modified without a thorough understanding then mistakes can be easily made. I have seen quite a few so-called F.O.I. "training manuals" over the years that have been copied and re-sold to brothers that speak on General Orders and give some, shall I say, "interesting" interpretations as to what each of them mean, but they really miss the mark because the language of military isn't understood. Officer of the Day and NCO were not explained and since I was an NCO in the Marine Corps, which has a long rich history, customs and traditions, I believe I am qualified to explain such. Now, we know that Master Fard Muhammad was born February 26, 1877, but the U. S. Marine Corps was established November 10, 1775, in Philadelphia, Pennsylvania, a little over 100 years before the birth of our Savior and 155 years before he (Master Fard) revealed himself to the Lost-Found Muslims in North America. So, before I go into the origin and history of the NCO, let's first examine the General Orders of the Marine Corps which go as follows:

General Orders, United States Marine Corps

1. To take charge of this post and all government property in view.

2. To walk my post in a military manner, keeping always on the alert and observing everything that takes place within sight or hearing.

3. To report all violations of orders I am instructed to enforce.

4. To repeat all calls from posts more distant from the guardhouse than my own.

5. To quit my post only when properly relieved.

6. To receive, obey and pass on to the sentry who relieves me all orders from the Commanding Officer, Officer of the Day, and officers and noncommissioned officers of the guard only.

7. To talk to no one except in the line of duty.

8. To give the alarm in case of fire or disorder.

9. To call the corporal of the guard in any case not covered by instructions.

10. To salute all officers and all colors and standards not cased.

11. To be especially watchful at night, and during the time for challenging, to challenge all persons on or near my post and to allow no one to pass without proper authority.

Now, I won't waste time listing the General Orders of the F.O.I. as, looking at the above, the similarities can be seen, so I will take this opportunity to direct your attention to what was changed. Why? Because the Most Hon. Elijah Muhammad said that when we study the circumstances surrounding the birth or origin of a thing we can determine the nature of that thing, and if the F.O.I. continue repeating General Orders of which they have no knowledge or understanding of their origin or meaning then they will never understand the nature of the present confusion or how these General Orders are significant to duty or how to truly make them relevant. So, as some of the General Orders are taken from the Marine Corps General Orders verbatim I will focus on the ones that were changed beginning with the 1st General Order and proceed from there:

1st General Order

"To take charge of this post and all government property in view" was changed to "all temple property in view" which can easily be understood as the word "government" implied United States Government/corporation (The U.S. is a corporation). And of course, the true "temple" is the physical human body which puts this General Order in a better perspective when considering taking charge, otherwise can be called "self-

determination," but the original order states "property in view" meaning what is visible to the eye and the mind cannot be seen, neither can the spirit, but they are manifested through action. The word *'charge'* is from Old French *chargier*, c. 1200, meaning "to load, to burden," as a verb it means "responsibility, burden."

2nd General Order

"To walk my post in a military manner, keeping always on the alert and observing everything that takes place within sight or hearing" was changed to walking in a "perfect manner" and the rest was omitted. But, I heard the Hon. Louis Farrakhan say in a lecture some years ago when speaking on the 2nd General Order that "...and we used to say keeping always on the alert and observing everything that takes place within sight or hearing." This implies that perhaps post-1975 this had been forgotten when certain individuals were putting together "training manuals" for the F.O.I. and listing the General Orders.

3rd General Order

"To report all violations of orders I am instructed to enforce" was kept the same, but what orders can we enforce except on ourselves? The word *'enforce'* means "to drive by physical force," also "make an effort; strengthen a place; compel." I take it that the latter definitions are what were implied when we adopted this order unless we have been given instructions to enforce orders which then brings into question competent authority.

4th General Order

"To repeat all calls from posts more distant from the guardhouse than my own" is a complicated one because the word "repeat" was changed to "report," and "guardhouse" was changed to "temple," as though someone tried to make this fit and make sense. But to understand the original meaning of this order one must understand that this order is relative to communications between guards at actual posts, be they Listening Posts (LP's) or Observation Posts (OP's), during a time when there were no electronic communications which would make distance a factor and repeating calls more distant from the guardhouse necessary. So an observation post (OP) where a guard was stationed which was far away from the main guardhouse wherein a sentry may have observed enemy smoke or signs of danger and would shout back towards a post closer to the guardhouse would have to be "repeated" in order for that message or warning to be

communicated back to the guardhouse. And who is at the guardhouse? The Corporal or Sergeant of the Guard, also known as an NCO, is at the guardhouse. This partially explains why "noncommissioned officers of the guard" is mentioned in General Order #6). Even as communications developed and advanced with telegraphs and radios, though the distance of communications improved, there is still limitations and some information with short-wave radios would have to be repeated between posts if the furthest post was out of communications range of the guardhouse. So the word "repeat " being changed to "report" may make sense to the civilian-minded (or non-Marine) person, or the one who borrowed from the Marine Corps General Orders but it is garble to a Marine.

6th General Order

"To receive, obey and pass on to the sentry who relieves me all orders from the commanding officer, officer of the day, and officers and noncommissioned officers of the guard only" has a word changed and a word omitted. The word "sentry" was changed to "sentinel" which isn't really a big deal at all since they both come from the same root word and mean essentially the same thing. However, the words "and officers" was omitted in the F.O.I. General Orders and perhaps the person who adopted these General Orders thought that it was pretty clever to drop that, or perhaps they didn't understand why it was in the General Orders to begin with. What do I mean? Well, technically, according to the F.O.I. General Orders, there is no order that officers in the Nation of Islam have to be obeyed unless they are the 'Commanding Officer' or 'Officer of the Day' (OOD). And what is the 'Officer of the Day'? Many an interpretation has been given to this billet by non-military speaking persons who have no clue and misunderstandings have been the result. But this is not surprising as this is what happens when we adopt a language and names of which we do not understand the meaning. So for the uninitiated and uninformed, in the military, the 'Officer of the Day' is the term used to describe the one day guard duty assignment for an officer who would be put in charge over the guard and prisoners on a military installation. Just as the guard/watch duty would be rotated among the enlisted-ranked military personnel, it is done similarly amongst the officers. When I was assigned to 'Area Guard' for a month while stationed at Camp Lejeune, NC I had one day of guard duty and two days off because of the number of guards we had on staff at the time. During that one month assignment I cannot recall seeing the same officer on duty twice as on a daily basis the assignment changed from one 1st or 2nd Lieutenant to the next. And when standing guard/barracks duty as an NCO while stationed at Camp Pendelton, CA the Duty NCO reports to the 'Officer of the Day' and the regular guard personnel report to the Duty NCO each shift.

8th General Order

"To give the alarm in case of fire or disorder" was changed to "In case of disorder give the alarm" and what has never been defined is what constitutes "disorder" and sadly the question is often repeated during F.O.I. drill "And what is the alarm?" to which the reply of "Allah-u-Akbar" (God is the Greatest) shouted three times would be given. However, "Allah-u-Akbar" is one of the most oft-repeated expressions amongst Muslims worldwide, especially in an expression of jubilance, so to shout this three times and expect someone to perceive that there is disorder causes nothing but confusion.

10th General Order

"To salute all officers and all colors and standards not cased" of course was made the 11th General Order for the F.O.I. as one original General Order was added out of the twelve (that ONE original General Order being the F.O.I. General Order No. 9, *"To allow no one to commit a nuisance on or near my post").* But the words "all colors" was omitted from this order and perhaps, once again, whomever adopted this was not aware of the term *'colors'* as it pertains to military language, or thought it was clever to drop this as well. Or, maybe they did happen to know this particular term and found that it was not applicable to the military, or military training, of the Nation of Islam. But I have yet to meet one F.O.I. who knows what a *"standard"* is and what the term *"not cased"* means. The military term *'colors'* (or colours) refers to the flag adopted by a particular military regiment (a Regiment consists of 2-4 battalions). This regimental flag was usually awarded to a regiment by a Head-of-State during a ceremony, usually for some distinguished service in battle(s) or campaigns by that particular regiment. So these flags would be held in high regard and treated with reverence and would bear the markings or symbols of achievements of said regiment in addition to names of battles inscribed on them. "Colors" are also organizational (also called a "ceremonial flag") as each military branch of service of the United States has its own "colors" which are carried by a Color Guard and can be seen at the military parades, civilian parades or at the beginning of major sporting events where-in you may see a Joint Color Guard composed of a representative of each branch of service. One Color Guard member carries the National flag and the others carry the "colors" of their organization (Marines, Navy, Army, Air Force & Coast Guard). There is a little more history to "colors" as it pertains to the battlefield but since it was omitted I will not bother to go into that. With regard to "standards not cased," a military "standard" is similar to "colors" with the exception that it is carried by cavalry (on horse) or vehicle. So basically, when "colors" are mounted on a vehicle (or carried by horseman) it is referred to as a "standard." As we don't have a cavalry (horse-riding) unit and we don't have a regimental flag (or battle/campaign flag) then leaving the word "standard" in the General Order and

omitting "colors" is confusing as they are both describing the same type of flag, the difference being one is carried on foot and the other is carried on a vehicle (or horse). And "not cased" refers to the covering put over the flag when it is rolled up, and has nothing to do with a flag in a display "case" as I have heard some individuals try to explain. I know many think that the flag of the Nation of Islam represented by the sun, moon, and star is a "standard," but simply refer to the Most Hon. Elijah Muhammad's book *'The Flag of Islam'* and find one page, paragraph, or sentence wherein he refers to our national flag as a "standard." You will not find it. Again, a "standard," as it relates to this General Order refers to a regiment's (or military organization) colors that are mounted on a vehicle. The U.S. Navy refers to this flag as an "ensign" when flown on Navy vessels. I hope this discrepancy is clear now.

11th General Order

"To be especially watchful at night, and during the time for challenging, to challenge all person on or near my post and to allow no one to pass without proper authority" of course became the 12th General Order for the F.O.I. and the bulk of this order was omitted, sadly. As, other than the military veterans, no one is versed in what a "challenge" is, the history of challenging, or how to challenge and why it is necessary with regards to guard duty or standing post.

The Non-Commissioned Officer (NCO)

Now this portion may offend some veterans of the Army (or other branches of service), but when I speak about the NCO, or noncommissioned officer, in order to give you the best example, I have to speak about the rank and file Corporals and Sergeants that are considered the "backbone" of the United States Marine Corps as there is no branch of service of the United States Armed Forces with a better example of what an NCO of the highest standards is with a richer history than the Marine NCO. But in any branch of service, the NCOs are the ones who MAKE IT HAPPEN AND GET THE JOB DONE! They are the trainers, the leaders, the Platoon Sergeants, the Drill Instructors, the counselors, the problem solvers, the hardest of the hardcore, roughest, meanest and fiercest fighters and warriors of the Marine Corps (and Army). They are the examples of the *primary and secondary objectives of military leadership* which is *'mission accomplishment'* and *'troop welfare'* because they lead by example and as supervisors they never ask, expect nor demand of those junior to them to do anything they would not do themselves. They are the vital link in the chain of command between the "private soldiers" or lower enlisted ranks and the officers. In the Marine Corps, when an officer wants something done, he tells a Sergeant or Corporal what he wants and the NCO makes it happen, and he doesn't have to tell the NCO "how" to get it done because they are experienced at making things happen. They are highly respected both by juniors and seniors, and of course I could go on and on about the Marine NCOs traditions, customs, courtesies, etc. But, I will just take time to explain why they are referred to as "noncommissioned" officers.

An officer's commission (as I explain in Volumes 1 & 2) is bestowed on them by the representatives of Congress and is indefinite (unless they fail to advance in their officer development cycle or fail to adhere to ethics), whereas an enlisted personnel's time in service is limited to their 2-6 year enlistment contract. After 2 or 3 years of enlisted service and depending on the nature of the time served along with their proficiency and conduct marks an enlisted person attains the pay-grade of E-4, which is the rank of Corporal (and I'm speaking specifically about the Marines as the Army has "Specialists"). At this point they become a noncommissioned officer and assume more leadership roles as squad leaders and trainers. The next rank up is Sergeant and after said rank they become Staff-NCOs (E-6 to E-9). Although the NCOs are junior to the officers in rank, they are the trainers of the officer candidates as they are the most experienced and the commissioned officers are well-advised to heed and seek counsel with their NCOs in the field, as experience (and those with it) is the best teacher.

So why is the NCO not mentioned in the Supreme Wisdom Lessons by Master Fard Muhammad to His Servant the Honorable Elijah Muhammad in the Wilderness of North America? Because the terminology comes from the U.S. Military and NOT Master Fard Muhammad, as I stated earlier, hence it is mentioned in the General Orders that we adopted from the U.S. Marines. And yet and still there are those who say we don't do like that so-called "Devil's military." So in the Nation of Islam, the closest we would have to what could be considered the equivalent of an NCO would be the squad leaders. I know some have tried to explain this as such in the inadequate "training manuals" that have been sold to the F.O.I. in the past but the problem is NCO (noncommissioned officer) refers to the military ranks of Corporal and Sergeant and "squad leader" is a position or billet, not a rank.

I pray, by Allah's (God) mercy, that I have been able to bring much clarity to any past confusion and misunderstanding of what a noncommissioned officer is and where the General Orders originated.

Section 3
Military Know-How

Chapter 5

The Children of Israel, Trials of Establishing a Service (Ministry) of Defense: Revisited, The Prequel

In Chapter 8 of '*On Military Science' Volume 2*, I spoke on the Children of Israel and their exploits throughout what I referred to as the "Promised Land Campaign" beginning in the Bible book of Joshua. I take this time to direct your attention to the biblical occurrences prior to the book of Joshua which led up to the Promised Land Campaign. I predicate this subject with the question "What were Joshua and Caleb doing during the 40 years the Children of Israel (COI) were made to wander in the wilderness while awaiting the old-minded rebels to die off before they began their campaign in the promised land of Canaan?" In order for me to answer this question in the way that my mind has resolved it let us examine the incident(s) that led up to the men of war ages 20 and up being denied entry into the promised land. It begins in the Bible book of Numbers. But first recall that in the Bible book of Exodus the Children of Israel begin their "exodus" out of the biblical Egypt after 430 years (Exodus 12:41). For us, the modern-day Children of Israel, the year 1955 marks the 400th year since the arrival of the first slaves/captives brought to American soil on the ship christened "Jesus" captained by one Sir John Hawkins (or Hopkins). This 400 year mark brings to light that we, the so-called Negros or Lost-Found Nation of Islam, are indeed the fulfillment of the promise given to Abraham (Abram) in the Bible book of Genesis 15:13-14:

13) And he said unto Abram, Know of a surety that thy seed shall be a stranger in a land that is not theirs, and shall serve them; and they shall afflict them four hundred years.

14) And also that nation, who they shall serve, will I judge: and afterward shall they come out with great substance. (KJV)

As there is no record of any other people being brought to a strange land and serving another people and being afflicted by that people they serve for four hundred years besides us the point is moot to wrestle with as to who/whom this scripture is describing today. Adding 30 years to that 400 year date (1555-1955) would bring us to the year 1985. And we know that this is the year that the Hon. Louis Farrakhan gave his 'Power At Last Forever' speech launching the P.O.W.E.R (People Organized Working for Economic Rebirth) products and an avenue to begin our economic "exodus" since the Hon. Louis Farrakhan's efforts to rebuild the work of the Most Hon. Elijah Muhammad began. Continuing with the biblical Children of Israel, by Exodus Chapter 13 the COI are being pursued by Pharaoh and his army and the "Lord" grants the COI victory by drowning the Pharaoh and his armies in the Red Sea. Moses and the COI sing a song of praise and proclaim that the "Lord" (Yahweh) is a man of war, and so continues their exodus.

One thing the Children of Israel seem to do best at this point is murmur, and they do A LOT of murmuring, from the Bible book of Exodus all the way through Leviticus and Numbers (not unlike today either). To *murmur* is to express discontent by grumbling and complaining. And in the course of their murmuring, which initially were complaints about food and the lack thereof, God grants them blessings of "manna" to eat for 40 years up until they reach Canaan (Exo. 16:35), and God grows weary of their murmurings as they continuously find something to complain about throughout the books of Exodus to Leviticus. In the 17th Chapter of Exodus Joshua is chosen to pick men to lead into battle against Amalek, wherein this is the first battle of the COI while they are on the run/exodus, and as long as Moses maintains his arms raised the COI prevail over the Amaleks. Chapter 20 finds Moses atop mount Sinai and God talking directly to him laying down the laws.

Fast-forward to the book of Numbers, which opens in the second month of the second year after the COI's exodus, a census (count, hence the book title "Numbers") is taken from each of the twelve tribes and then a military draft is instituted of all able-bodied males of ages 20 and up with the exception of the Levites, also known as priests (ministers). The Levites were required to take their men ages 30 to 50 to perform the work and service required in the tabernacle (Num. 4:23), otherwise could be ministers and secretaries by today's understanding of the duties they were to perform. The total number of males comprising the army of the COI, according to Leviticus 1:46 and 2:32, ends up being 603,550 (6+3+5+5= 19). The 12 tribes are organized into camps, each with their own ensign (unit flag), arranged in ranks, and captains from each tribe are designated (Num. 2:3, 5, 7, 10, 12, 14, 18, 20, 22, 25, 27, 29).

By the 11th Chapter of Numbers we find the Children of Israel, yet again, complaining to the point that the anger of the Lord was kindled. According to Num. 11:1, the fire of the Lord *"burnt among them, and consumed them that were in the uttermost parts of the camp."* The people cry to Moses and Moses prays to the Lord to quench the fire. The COI then cry some more over food and whining over why God brought them out of Egypt as they were suffering and God comes down in a "cloud" and gives the spirit to seventy elders and the elders began to prophesy in the tabernacles non-stop with the exception of two of them (who remain in the camps) and Joshua pleads on their behalf to Moses. This, followed by the Lord blessing the people with quail to eat but all that eat the quail are plagued by the wrath of the Lord. Could this be the Most Hon. Elijah Muhammad saying that we COULD eat meat (after numerous followers complained and asked what about the consumption of meat), in *How to Eat to Live*, but also saying that we SHOULD be vegetarian? As there are many Muslims who are suffering from all kinds of ailments and illnesses from eating dead animal flesh and not adhering strictly to the tenets of our dietary law. And by the 13th Chapter Moses is commanded to send out men to "search the land" (reconnoiter) of Canaan. This is where Caleb, the son of Jephunneh of the tribe of Judah, comes in along with 11 others representing each of the 12 tribes of the Children of Israel as scouts.

So in Numbers 13:17 the scouts are sent out with instructions from Moses (the Commander-in-Chief) on which areas to conduct their reconnaissance and what to bring back (the fruit of the land). By 13:25 they return after 40 days and deliver their After-Action Report (AAR) to Moses, Aaron, and the Children of Israel, and showed them the fruits from the land which they acquired. The scouts report the land is flowing with "milk and honey" (13:27), but that the people that dwell in the land are strong with great cities that are walled (13:28).

By this report, I interject; this would imply the necessity for what is called 'Seige Warfare', which is a difficult military task second only to 'Amphibious Warfare'. Their report continues with the locations of the different peoples (Amalekites, Hittites, Jebusites, Amorites, Canaanites, and the children of Anak). Three of the enemies dwelling in the mountains, which presents serious problems such as the issues faced currently by troops fighting in Afghanistan engaged in 'Mountain Warfare,' and the Canaanites dwelled by the sea and the coast of Jordan, which would possibly necessitate engaging in Amphibious Warfare (establishing a beachhead and so forth) or make the "avenues of approach" to the Canaanites limited (as they didn't have a navy or boats) which would mean the Children of Israel would be highly exposed or lessen the chance for any surprise attacks. Now, as the congregations clamored during this debriefing, Caleb proposes that they go into the land despite the odds and difficulties and seize the initiative and occupy the land (13:30). But the other scouts disagreed and believed that the people of Canaan were stronger (13:31), and then according to 13:32-33:

32) And they brought up an evil report of the land which they had searched unto the children of Israel, saying, The land, through which we have gone to search it, is a land that eateth up the inhabitants thereof; and all the people that we saw in it are men of great statute.

33) And there we saw giants, the sons of Anak, which come of the giants; and we were in our own sight as grasshoppers, and so we were in their sight.

This report was followed by more murmuring from the Children of Israel against Moses and Aaron, along with crying and lamenting over leaving Egypt, to the point they conferred to make another captain to lead them and return to Egypt (14:4). It is at this point that Joshua (obviously siding with Caleb) and Caleb express their frustration and beckon to the people to not be afraid and exercise faith that the Lord will deliver the land to them if they don't rebel (14:9). The Children of Israel disagreed to the point of suggesting stoning Joshua and Caleb, and the Lord appears in the tabernacle of the congregation and questions Moses as to how long will the people provoke him (the Lord) and how long until they truly believe even after all of the signs God showed them. **Then God gets angry and threatens to kill the Children of Israel (14:12) and**

Moses pleads and prays on their behalf for God to spare their lives. God pardons Moses but by 14:23 decrees,

23) Surely they shall not see the land which I sware unto their fathers, neither shall any of them that provoked me see it.

24) But my servant Caleb, because he had another spirit with him, and hath followed me fully, him will I bring into the land whereinto he went; and his seed shall possess it.

God refers to the Children of Israel as an "evil congregation" in verse 27 (KJV) where he says, *"How long shall I bear with this evil congregation, which murmur against me? I have heard the murmurings of the children of Israel, which they murmur against me."* And God says that as the children of Israel have spoken in his ears so shall He do to them and promises that all of them who murmured, ages 20 and up, will die in the wilderness (14:29) except Joshua and Caleb (14:30). The Lord promises them in 14:33-34:

33) And your children shall wander in the wilderness forty years, and bear your whoredoms, until your carcasses be wasted in the wilderness.

34) After the number of days in which ye searched the land, even forty days, each day for a year, shall ye bear your iniquities, even forty years, and ye shall know my breach of promise.

And now I close this with the following answer to the initial question I asked pertaining to what Joshua and Caleb were doing during the 40 years of the Children of Israel wandering in the wilderness, and my answer is that THEY WERE TRAINING. In order for them to have executed with success the 'Promised Land Campaign' I spoke of in Chapter 8 of 'On Military Science', Volume 2, there would have to have been proper military training. The Bible book of Proverbs 23:7 says, *"For as he thinketh in his heart, so is he: Eat and drink, saith he to thee; but his heart is not with thee."* I say that, **just as a man thinks in his heart so IS he, as a man is taught and trained so DOES he, and right action is a reflection of right training.** This cannot be overlooked or dismissed, so as the Hon. Louis Farrakhan stated and still has not recanted that he does not have "one military mosque" we must re-examine the military training (and lack thereof) of the men who belong to Islam here in the wilderness of North America (I will cover that in 'How to Build A Military Mosque'). So just as Joshua and Caleb represented the minority of the Children of Israel who were ready and willing to take the Promised Land, so too are there those who are and have been ready and willing to establish a proper Ministry of Defense for our beloved Nation of Islam to establish a land of our own within the land that our forefathers built, slaved, toiled, and sacrificed for.

Mind you, the Children of Israel had been organized into ranks of fighting men and designated captains but what was the training of these captains? It is my conviction that there was little to none as the majority of them had been slaves in the biblical Egypt prior to their exodus out of Egypt which mimics the conditions today. This is why, when it came to the scouting report presented, Caleb was the only scout who weighed the pros and cons, considered the **S**ize, **A**ctivity, **L**ocation(s), **U**nit (strengths/weaknesses), **T**ime (and what must be done), and **E**nemy activity (the acronym SALUTE is used in reporting reconnaissance intelligence gathered) and recommended that they seize the initiative and engage the enemies in Canaan. Joshua, having some military experience as well, was the only other soldier to back Caleb's recommendation and assessment. Recall that Joshua was commissioned by Moses to recruit fighting men to contend with Amalek back in Exodus 17:9-10, and Joshua did so successfully (Exod. 17:13). The rest of the captains were not designated captains until the Bible book of Numbers, and they didn't have any real military training from which to draw from and so they were opposed to engaging in warfare though they may have spoken of war before. They now murmured in their tents against Moses, Aaron, Caleb and Joshua. So after being sentenced by God to continue wandering the wilderness for 40 years and continuously annoying God by their blatant displays of a lack of discipline, military bearing, adherence to the laws of Moses (given to him by God), and failure to keep the commandments (or commands), I am convinced this was all a reflection of and a result of their lack of military training. I have stated before that training is the cornerstone of readiness, and to me it is obvious that Joshua and Caleb (and the youthful soldiers that followed them) continued training during the 40 years of wandering as all of the old-minded, murmuring warriors and people of the Children of Israel died off, otherwise they (Joshua and Caleb) would not have been ready and as successful in their battles they engaged in west of the River Jordan. And we are west of the "River Jordan" which, subsequently, is also the name for the great current across the Atlantic Ocean which was traveled by slave ships during the 16th-19th centuries. And the moral of my relaying this biblical story is to emphasize for us to focus on training instead of complaining (murmuring). Again, **as a man is taught and trained so DOES he, right action is a reflection of right training.** Thank you for reading.

Chapter 6

How to Build a Military Mosque

In examining the words of the Hon. Louis Farrakhan wherein he stated several years ago that he does not have "one military mosque," in this expression the word *military* is used as an adjective. The *Online Etymological Dictionary* states that military (adj.) is from mid-15 century, from M. French *militaire* (14c.), from Latin *militaris* "of soldiers or war, of military service, warlike," from *miles* (gen. *militis*) "soldier." Generally, when a person states what they do not have it is implied that they need or want such that they do not have. If the Hon. Louis Farrakhan had stated that he did not have one mosque, I'm quite sure that immediately the Council of Laborers would have met and inquired as to who had architectural skills, construction skills, and such persons or commercial companies would have been consulted and recruited from within the entire organization of the Nation of Islam, along with carpenters, electricians, plumbers, interior decorators, and any other trade required to build such a mosque. Why did this not happen with reference to the "military mosque"? As I pointed out in my thesis presented in '*On Military Science*' Volume 1, the reasons why people fail to do what they are supposed to do (as presented in the book '*Coaching for Improved Work Performance*' by F.F. Fournies), they don't know 1) what to do, 2) how to do, 3) why they should, 4) there are obstacles in their way, and an occasional fifth reason 5) they simply don't care enough to do. The fact that the Hon. Louis Farrakhan has yet to recant that statement proves that we have continued to demonstrate that we do not know what to do, how to do, why we should, etc. I know in many cities the challenge to build such a military mosque was taken on and there were those who thought that by doing more close-order drill they would produce such a mosque. And so in every F.O.I. class men formed up in ranks and someone who thought they knew drill or called themselves drill instructors barked commands of "left face!", "right face!", "about face!" and then some "trick" drill commands such as "flank-ways to rear, march!". And let's not forget "mark-time, march!" And so the men marked time, stomping and strutting in place, turning to the left and right and never moving forward, sweating, shouting cadences, moving their feet at a fast pace and going absolutely nowhere fast.

What would be the purpose of a "military mosque"? Military represents organization, training, and the ability to execute or carry out commands, successfully accomplish any given mission, and do so in a collective and cooperative manner as a unit with technical and tactical proficiency. It also represents an organization with the ability to defend and counter-attack any aggressive opposition that arises and attacks, along with an ability to be the maintainers and peace-keeping force. To say that we do not have one military mosque is to imply we do not have the above-mentioned. And so it is my intention to cover 1) what to do, 2) how to do, 3) why we should, 4) how to overcome the obstacles (as well as identify what those obstacles are), and 5) why we should care.

What To Do

First, there are plenty of U.S. Armed Forces veterans who are registered Believers within the ranks of the Nation of Islam, both male and female, these persons should be considered the go-to people and consulted with regard to their military training and specific expertise, as everyone didn't do or have the same job (Military Occupational Specialty/MOS) in the military. From those veterans find out who were the officers and non-commissioned officers (NCOs). The NCOs are really the ones who will make things happen as they were considered (and proven to be) the backbone of the military. The officers will be most effective at organizing and logistics. The NCOs will be most effective at training, communication with the men, and execution of the primary and secondary objectives of leadership (Mission Accomplishment, and Troop Welfare). Also, find out what branch of service (Army, Navy, Air Force, Marines, Coast Guard, National Guard) and MOS these veterans served in, as an NCO or officer who was over Supply or Administration will not have the know-how nor expertise of an NCO or officer who served as a Basic Infantryman or Special Forces. As each branch of service has a different mission, this too will determine the effectiveness of the veteran, and must also be considered. The Army's mission is not the same as the Navy (or other branches) and therefore the training is different, although the core leadership values, traits and principles will be the same in all of the branches, as well as the Army is currently conducting combined-arms training with the Marines and they have produced such combined training manuals.

What also needs to be done is to establish guidelines, according to the Hon. Louis Farrakhan, the teachings of the Most Hon. Elijah Muhammad, and the tenets of our Islamic doctrine as to what kind of military and Ministry of Defense we will establish which will then in turn give us our mission and dictate our training to accomplish such. We know from *'The Meaning of F.O.I.'* that we are not to be trained *"in the manner of the army of the devil"* (pg 9) or *"as an army of killers"* (pg 10), and because of this those without military training at all frowned upon those who had it and immediately rejected and negated any and all expertise and training of those who were veterans. Without having a proper understanding of what aspects of their military training are good and can be used, such persons who rejected that training have metaphorically stripped an engine and drive-train of a vehicle of the parts that make it drive and ignorantly kept what they thought was essential which drives us nowhere (perhaps part of the reason we drill and mark-time and never move forward, more on that later). I gave examples of just a few countries that have Ministries of Defense in Volume 2 of *'On Military Science'* that may be examined and studied closer to gain better insight and understanding as to what a Ministry of Defense is comprised of.

How To Do

Once the Armed Forces veterans have been determined, designate those who were Marines or Army Special Forces, and make these the captains, lieutenants and drill instructors according to their military expertise. I can speak on behalf of the Marine veterans, and say that it is necessary to understand that everyone that was in the Marines was not an NCO or a "grunt" (Basic Rifleman). That being the case, it cannot be assumed that just because a person was or claims to have been in the Marine Corps that they automatically have leadership skills or qualifications. There must be consideration for what their MOS was and how long they were enlisted and whether or not they were considered to be a "squared away" Marine. But for those who were squared away, combat trained, as well as trained as NCOs (also Staff NCOs), from this lot you will find the most effective leaders, teachers, and trainers to pool from. We also have a brother whom I know personally and have been trained by (in the martial arts) who was a Drill Instructor at Drill Instructor School for the Marine Corps, meaning he trained and produced the very same Marine Corps Drill Instructors who train and produce Marines (from recruits), a Drill Instructor OF the Drill Instructors. It doesn't get any higher than that as far as training expertise goes. So I know there are a few others who may have had similar training and experience.

From these Marine NCO and Army Special Forces veterans you will establish the best and most effective captains and lieutenants in the Nation of Islam. Make the other veterans the squad leaders and team leaders. In a short period of time, as the duty of the lieutenant is to teach the private soldier; also train them, according to our Supreme Wisdom lesson, these lieutenants will be able to train the squad leaders to become lieutenants and team leaders to become squad leaders as the ranks grow. The veteran squad leaders and team leaders will be the best examples to those who never had any type of real military training and experience before. And the ranks will grow fast! Organizing from the ground up, assign three men to one Team Leader, and three teams will comprise a Squad. The senior most Team Leader is to be made the Squad Leader. This means there will be a total of 12 men making up a squad. The three team members report to the one Team Leader, and the two junior Team Leaders report to the Squad Leader. The Marine Corps adopted this from the Chinese after they sent military liaisons to China, this is where the Marine Corps adopted the expression "*gung-ho*" from which means *work* (gung) *together* (ho). The Chinese found that it was easier to manage and coordinate things and people in 3's. So three teams make up a squad, and three squads (or possibly four squads) make up a platoon. Make the lieutenants platoon leaders and have the squad leaders report to the lieutenant. A "platoon Sergeant" can also be established and this person would be like the executive officer of the platoon leader (lieutenant). This is how it is done in the military, and the platoon Sergeant RUNS the platoon and looks after the men (troop welfare) and keeps them on task.

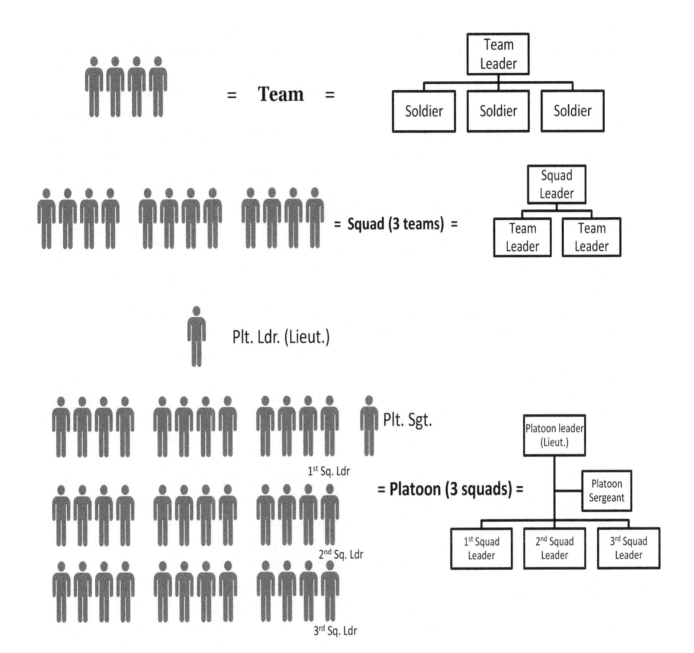

So each platoon will be comprised of 36 men (12 x 3) or 42 men (12 x 4) depending on if 3 or 4 squads are used and the platoon leader will make the 37th or 43rd man. For those who like to refer to the *Holy Qur'an* when they see numbers, the 37th Surah of the *Holy Qur'an* is entitled 'Al-Saffat' meaning "Those Ranging in Ranks", and the 43rd Surah is entitled 'Zhukhruf' meaning "Gold," which is the color of the insignia of 2nd Lieutenants and Majors in the armed forces. And again, the Chinese found that it is easier to maintain and control things in 3's, so I tend to go with the 3 squads comprising a platoon. Once the number of men are found sufficient to comprise a platoon (3 squads), then designate a platoon leader (lieutenant).

For some reason non-militarily trained persons in charge have made lieutenants into squad leaders in the Nation of Islam and then the past trend has been to make a person a lieutenant and have that person call and stay in contact with everyone in their squad. This is too taxing on one individual, as one individual would have to make 10 or more phone calls to keep track of the men in his squad. The better method is to do the above-described, which is the reverse of how things have been done, and have 3 men report to 1 man and carry that trend up through the echelons of team leader, squad leader and platoon leader. This is much more organized and more efficient and reflects military.

As the ranks of the mosques grow and there are more and more men then the above is repeated until there are 2 and 3 platoons, each with a lieutenant over them. At the regional mosque level this will be easier to implement and maintain organization. Once 3 platoons have been organized you now have what is called a "company." In the military, captains (Army, Marine Corps) are Company Commanders. The Navy has 1st Officers, and their 1st Officers are second in command under a Naval Captain which is equivalent to the Army/Marine Corps rank of Colonel (pay grade O-6, pay grades are O-1 through O-10 with 10 being the highest). But since we have no naval vessels which we operate aboard or command I have never understood why the term "1st Officer" has been used in the Nation of Islam and it seems that 1st Lieutenant (the rank below a Captain) has been interchanged with 1st Officer and there is a difference. In the military the next in command under the Captain (Company Commander) is known as the Executive Officer (XO). Generally, the platoon leaders are 2nd and 1st Lieutenants and the senior most 1st Lieutenant is the XO, they may also be the platoon leader over a 4th platoon which would be designated a "special weapons" platoon. This would be the platoon with all of your scout snipers, heavy machine-gunners, mortar-men, and so forth but since we do not carry weapons I see no reason to have such a platoon unless it would comprise of those who are "specially trained/training" in the martial arts/sciences, or those with special skills such as doctors or EMTs, scientists, engineers, and so forth. So to recap, the 3 team members report to the Team Leader, the 2 team leaders report to the senior team leader designated as the Squad Leader. And they should always form up in ranks accordingly with the Squad Leader to the extreme right (lining up tallest man to shortest is the elementary way of forming a unit when there are no designated leaders). The 3 squad leaders report to the platoon leader (lieutenant), or platoon Sergeant if it has been deemed necessary to have such a position, in such a case the platoon Sergeant would report solely to the platoon leader. The 3 platoon leaders would then report to the XO and the XO reports directly to the Captain.

Company = 3 platoons =

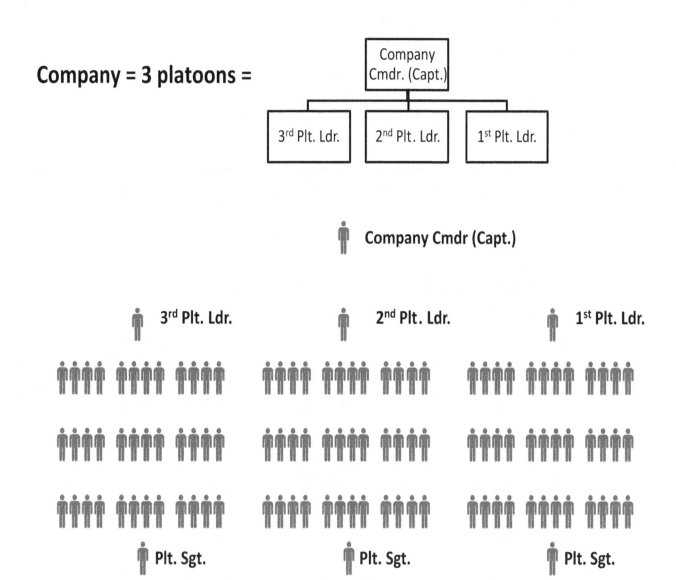

In the event that the ranks number such that there are enough men to form more than one company then another captain would be designated, 3 companies make up what is known as a "battalion" and at this stage you would have a battalion commander and a battalion XO as well as a staff which would be divided into what are called "S-shops". These "S-shops" ("S" meaning staff) in the military are designated S1-S5, there are more depending on the needed functions of larger military units and joint operations. The battalion commander usually carries the rank of Lieutenant Colonel (Lt. Col.) and the XO is usually a Major, there are exceptions however. Back to the S-shops, in the military the staff personnel are divided into the following with an officer over each function:

Executive officer (XO) – duties and responsibilities are tailored to the wishes and desires of the commander, but also include the following four major tasks:

- Coordination of all staff functions
- Assumes command in the absence of the commander
- Prepares for future operations of the unit
- Makes sure that liaison and coordination are conducted with higher headquarters by the appropriate staff sections as needed.

S1 – This officer is called the "Adjutant" in the military and is responsible for preparing the personnel estimate and providing input on the effects of personnel status on operations as well as the following:

- Maintain unit strength reports
- Process wounded and killed in action as well as prisoners of war (POW).
- Maintain unit morale (I also interject "moral conduct").
- Maintains discipline, law, and order.

S2 – This is the "Intelligence officer" and is considered the driving force for all military operations. This consideration is due to the fact that, the S3 cannot plan for tactical operations with any degree of success without timely, accurate intelligence and current estimates of enemy courses of action and locations. The Intelligence officer fulfills this vital role by:

- Maintaining current intelligence information
- Developing and interpreting intelligence information
- Gathering intelligence information
- Determining likely and suspected enemy targets (what the enemy may attack)
- Preparing for future operations

There is much more items the S2 uses to accomplish his tasks but for the sake of brevity I will not list such at this writing, but it can be summed up with about 19 points.

S3 – This is the "Operations and training officer" whose duty it is to prepare the operations estimates and recommend to the commander the actions to be taken. His tactical plan is driven by the estimates, predictions, and information supplied by the S2 and both the S2 and S3 work closely together in order to successfully support the mission. Overall, the Operations and training officer's duties include:

- Receiving and sending initial unit or attachment dispositions
- Monitoring the tactical situation
- Analyzing, interpreting, and recommending courses of action
- Interacting and coordinating with other staffs
- Maintaining communications

- Preparing for future operations
- Supervising training

S4 – This is the "Logistics officer" who is responsible for advising the commander on all logistical matters, determining supply and other service support requirements. The Logistics officer prepares the logistical estimate and logistical administrative plans, and also accomplishes the following:

- Maintains equipment readiness reports
- Monitors support of units or attachments
- Monitors the tactical situation (in the field/battlefield)
- Supervises use of transportation assets (to include fuel consumption and maintenance)
- Prepares for future operations
- In charge of supply and re-supply of necessary caches for units in action.

S5 – This is the "Civil-military operations officer" who has a major role when it comes to dealing with the civilian population. The S5 prepares civil affairs estimates and portions of the operations orders, and as all operations have civil affairs value, the S5 ensures this value supports the overall military goals. The S5 accomplishes this by doing the following:

- Advising, assisting, and making recommendations that relate to civil affairs
- Making recommendations to ensure operations are consistent with overall military goals
- Coordinating and implementing the civil affairs tasks of the military units.[14]

The above S-shops could easily be adopted to better coordinate the efforts of the F.O.I., the S5/Civil-military operations officer would be equivalent to those persons who have and maintain good ties with community leaders, clergy, and other persons and organizations outside of the Nation of Islam who are supporters of the Hon. Louis Farrakhan. The other Staff officer positions and functions should be easy to understand, relate and adapt to the goals and functions necessary within the Nation of Islam in order to establish a proper Ministry of Defense.

Why We Should

As the Hon. Louis Farrakhan stated in '*The Meaning of F.O.I.*', "*The old military training of the FOI was wrong in several respects. And that is condemned by God and the Messenger and by myself. The old military training must be thrown out of the*

---

[14] US Army Counterguerrilla Operations Handbook, Dept. of the Army, appendix I (I-1 through I-4)

window because that was not a training to save our people" (page 9). The "several respects" that was wrong must be understood, it does not mean that ANY AND ALL MILITARY TRAINING must be thrown out of the window. It means that any training that has nothing to do with helping us to become an army of Saviours and be able to save our people must be thrown out of the window. If this were not so then we should stop drilling and doing facing movements and saluting altogether, because we do them all exactly as the so-called devil's military with the exception that we turn our head before facing. And there is nothing in nature that moves doing facing movements squarely, everything in nature that moves and turns does so in spirals, circles, arcs, or similar patterns. So a lack of understanding has caused us to produce no military mosque after all of this time. It was Captain Salim Muhammad who encouraged me to not throw any of the military manuals and training that I received away because he saw (as a veteran himself) that there were aspects of said training that could be utilized to ensure our success when we use such in the name of Allah and for the right purpose.

And so all of the armed forces veterans who came to the Nation of Islam were immediately checked by someone who had no training and told that "we don't do that devil's military" and they accepted such because most of the veterans were happy to get away from that military, and with good reason based on their experiences. However, if we were establishing a Muslim bakery or restaurant, we would not dismiss the culinary training, expertise, and experience of those Muslims who went to culinary schools owned by the so-called devils (as we do not have nor operate one of our own) and we would have a fine restaurant and bakery if we utilized such persons. The same as would be if we were establishing a trucking company, we wouldn't dismiss those who obtained commercial driver's licenses (CDLs) and had training, expertise, and experience from those who went to trucking schools owned and operated by the so-called devils (as we do not have nor operate one of our own), and we would have a fine trucking company if we utilized such persons. I could go on and on with similar examples, but the point is that if we are to establish such a military mosque then why not properly utilize those veterans with military training and experience to do so? Islam comes after all else fails and since we have failed at establishing a military mosque doing things the way they have been done by those who have been in charge, what other way is there to do it then? Again, according to the blueprint of the Most Hon. Elijah Muhammad in *Message to the Blackman in America*, we are supposed to:

1. *Recognize the necessity for unity and group operation (activities)*
2. *Pool your resources, physically as well as financially.*
3. *Stop wanton criticisms of everything that is black-owned and black-operated.*
4. *Keep in mind – jealousy destroys from within.*
5. *Observe the operations of the white man. He is successful. He makes no excuses for his failures. He works hard in a collective manner. You do the same.*

If there are six or eight Muslims with knowledge and experience of the grocery business - pool your knowledge, open a grocery store – and you work collectively and harmoniously, Allah will bless you with success.

If there are those with knowledge of dressmaking, merchandising, trades, maintenance – pool such knowledge. Do not be ashamed to seek guidance and instructions from the brother or sister who has more experience, education and training than you have had. Accept his or her assistance[15].

To the five points of the Messenger's blueprint I ask the following:

1. Who better understands unity and group operations than those Muslims who are veterans of the U.S. Armed Forces wherein they were constantly trained in and operated in military units conducting group and joint operations?
2. Who better understands how to pool resources (especially when they are limited) and how to improvise, adapt and overcome obstacles by utilizing such resources than the Muslims who are veterans of the armed forces?
3. At what point will there be a stop to wanton criticism (by those who have NO military training or experience) of those Muslims who have military training and experience in military operations?
4. Since jealousy destroys from within, has it been jealousy from those who have no military training that motivated them to speak ill of, dismiss, disregard, disrespect, and drive away those who are armed forces veterans?
5. In observing the operations of the white man, who besides the white man has a military that is successfully deployed all over the world working in a collective manner to achieve the political, industrial/commercial, and economic aims of their government?

We have not one military mosque because we failed to use, seek guidance and instructions from, and accept the assistance of the Muslims with knowledge and experience in military affairs, pooling their knowledge, experience, education, and training, and allowing them to work collectively and harmoniously, and this is why Allah has not blessed us with success in building a military mosque.

The Obstacles

Egotism, Envy, Jealousy, Entitlement, Greed, and Obstinacy, from my 20 years of observation, have been the root obstacles in our way disallowing us the opportunity to establish a proper Ministry of Defense. Misunderstanding is always at the root as well, and we cannot have understanding, or patience, where a comprehensive knowledge is

---

[15] *Message to the Blackman in America*, Hon. Elijah Muhammad, pg 174

lacking (just as with Moses following the Wiseman in the 18th Surah of the Holy Qur'an). Besides these, and of course the machinations of the Counter-Intelligence Program (COINTELPRO) which is still in operation as the enemy has us "all but like a church" still, there are no other obstacles that prevent us from building a military mosque because we have the expertise and man-power among us to do such. Those in leadership guilty of obstinacy, and any of the other illnesses or combination thereof, will end up like the captains and priests/ministers mentioned in the previous chapter referencing the biblical Children of Israel, meaning they will die off and the Joshua-and-Caleb-personas will continue training and eventually the 40 years of wandering sentenced by God against the murmuring Children of Israel will be up and we will successfully take the Promised Land and occupy the positions awaiting those of us who qualify ourselves.

It is prayer, study, fasting, and auditing that will enable us to overcome the above-mentioned obstacles, unless there are hearts hardened by Allah and He chooses to leave such persons blindly wandering on in their inordinacy like the Children of Israel sentenced to die off and not enter the Promised Land. Seeking assistance and guidance from those armed forces veterans who have experience in leadership, organizing, and training will be of benefit as well. Their entire training from day one of Basic Training, or Boot Camp, is based on overcoming obstacles, mentally, spiritually, and physically. This is why they are constantly tested and evaluated in physical training (obstacle courses, 3-plus mile runs, physical fitness, etc), battlefield tactics and combat maneuvers both daytime and nighttime with sleep deprivation (mental), and exercised repetitively in motivation (spiritual) in all of their tasks. What better persons to seek counsel and guidance from to overcome obstacles than the very veterans who are trained in overcoming obstacles?

Why We Should Care

It is said that you cannot be a true Muslim until you want for your brother and sister what you want for yourself. In order for us to become an army of Saviors we cannot perform in this capacity properly without caring and having an affinity for our people. Otherwise we will not be successful. In order for us to really want for others what we want for ourselves we must care, to *care* is to be anxious, grieve; to feel concern or interest, how can we pray and ask God to care for us when we do not demonstrate anxiety, grief, concern or interest over others? Inviting people to the mosque does not suffice as demonstration of concern, it is merely a start. Once they get to the mosque then what? When you invite others to your home it is proper to feed them and entertain them, but those who are invited to the mosque and who join onto the Nation of Islam are at that point babies in the faith. And there must be such institutions in place that can nurture, teach, and train the "child in faith" until maturity or the age where they can go off on their own. This is what has been demonstrated throughout the history of military training, and it is one of the reasons many who are veterans now were recruited into the armed forces, they knew they would be clothed, fed, sheltered, and trained in some skill and earn pay/allowance. This could and can be done in the Nation of Islam as well, properly pooling our resources will facilitate a way for us collectively to clothe, feed, shelter, and train the new join as well as the elders who have sacrificed for the cause of Islam.

Conclusion

And so when we address and institute the above-mentioned recommendations we will see the nucleus of a military mosque and proper Ministry of Defense formed. It cannot be dictated by those who have no military training or comprehensive knowledge, that has already been done and that is why we still do not have one military mosque in all of the Nation. If it could have been done as such then it already would have been done as such. Those who disagree would have a hard time proving otherwise as had it not been for the Hand of Allah in all of our affairs we would not have been successful in anything we have endeavored to do up to this time. To have a military mosque would mean that there would be proper training and execution of our mission in the most efficient time carried out in the most efficient manner and methodology by the most disciplined and organized body of trained soldiers as that is what "military" represents.

Chapter 7

How Officers Are Trained

I have written on what a commissioned officer is (*On Military Science... Vol. 1*) and in spite of what I thought were clear distinctions explained between a commissioned officer and non-commissioned officer there has still been some confusion expressed to me by officers within the Nation of Islam. This I attribute to the fact that, as I have stated before, every profession has its own language and there are those who don't know and have failed to learn the language of military which is part of the reason why the Hon. Louis Farrakhan still does not have one military mosque since the time he stated so around six years ago. Since that time many so-called officers have been stood up, many should have been sat down though they still remain in leadership positions, and numerous qualified persons continue to be overlooked. In the military, officers who fail to progress through what is called an "officer development cycle" and who also fail to perform to task as unit leaders are removed from those leadership positions after evaluation and assessment from their "fitness reports." In no way shape or form would a so-called Captain remain the Company Commander or Platoon Leader for any extended period of time beyond 18 months (on average) without displaying tactical and technical proficiency. I know, I know, "this isn't the Devil's military," and because it is not and due to the fact we have no written guidelines or regulations, let alone training, for officers in the Nation of Islam at present the only thing I can make any comparisons against is the so-called Devil's military until such is developed.

The Supreme Wisdom states that the duty of the Lieutenant (in the Nation of Islam) is to *"teach the private soldier; also train them."* Teach them what? Train them how? What is it that the one teaching should be knowledgeable of and what should they be trained in? In my DVD '*Military Science: The Purpose of Military Training*' (copyright 2011) I stated:

"The implication of teaching is to increase or expand the knowledge of a student, the desired or expected outcome of which is to aid the student with becoming wiser and technically proficient in a given field.

The implication of training is to guide the growth of the student toward specified goals, the desire or expected outcome being to increase the student's ability to act and perform more proficiently in a given field."

It is not enough for a student Minister or student Captain to stand before the Fruit of Islam and ask "who wants to be a Lieutenant?," deputize the volunteers and then unleash the unqualified onto the body of men with no knowledge or training. This is generally what has been done and yet and still the Hon. Louis Farrakhan doesn't have one military mosque. So instead of focusing on what we don't do, don't have, and don't know, perhaps it is best to shed light on what may be of interest to those who are desirous to know how officers are qualified and trained in the military before being commissioned.

Prerequisites for Officer Candidates

A person desirous of becoming a commissioned officer in any branch of service must first apply as an officer candidate to be trained at an accredited military institute, training academy, Platoon Leaders Class, Reserve Officer Training Corps (ROTC), or Officer Candidate School (OCS), Enlisted Commissioning Program (for enlisted Marines with a college degree), Meritorious Commissioning Program (Marine Corps), Marine Enlisted Commissioning Education Program (MECEP, Marine Corps) and there are strict requirements for each. There are also direct commissions for soldiers but these only apply to combat service support branches of the military for medical professionals, lawyers, and chaplains, in other words, they are not commissioned in the fighting units wherein he must be steeped in the knowledge of the troop leading procedures, how to create Operations Orders (OPORD), infantry tactics, land navigation, etc.

The word "candidate" is derived from the Latin word *candida* meaning "white" and stems from an ancient Rome practice wherein people running for political office would wear togas which were chalked and bleached white for their speeches in public. As white is the absence of color my interpretation of why a person is considered an officer "candidate" is because they are a blank slate when it comes to knowledge of military leadership, tactics, proficiency, and so forth. The same could be analogous to the white belt worn in the beginning phase and stages of martial arts training; it is no rank at all and represents a void of knowledge.

So each **officer candidate must** have a **high moral character**. They must be **academically sound** and cannot fail more than three written exams. During all phases of training they will serve in various command positions and have to achieve an overall satisfactory **leadership** rating. They must pass a physical examination and be deemed **medically sound**. And they must participate in regularly scheduled physical fitness and conditioning training and score the minimum requirements of their Physical Fitness Test (PFT) proving themselves **physically fit**, in addition to meeting weight standards. All of this is presented before a review board and a majority rule in favor of the applicant is accepted into Officer Candidate School.

Other requirements include:

- Education – they must have a four-year degree to be eligible to apply (or near the last year of obtaining their degree if they are enlisted seeking candidacy through an above-mentioned program).
- Letter of Recommendation – all candidates must have a letter of recommendation from an officer, preferably someone they have worked for before and with the rank of Captain or above.
- Security Clearance – they must have the ability to earn a security clearance. Their request can be denied for having been convicted in a U.S. court for a crime and

72

serving a prison sentence in excess of one year. It can also be denied for use or addiction to controlled substances (drugs/alcohol), being found mentally incompetent as determined by a Department of Defense approved health professional, being dishonorably discharged or dismissed from the armed forces, and even a bad credit history for any variety of reasons.

- Biography – One of the first assignments of an officer candidate is to write an autobiography focusing on the part of their life that led them to consider becoming an officer. Ideal biographies include vital statistics, special events and circumstances that led them to be who they are, as well as an explanation of what they will contribute to society once they gain OCS education and what they will contribute after completing training and gaining a commission.

TAC Method – Teach, Assess, Counsel

TAC officers (Army) and SNCO/NCOs (staff/non-commissioned officers) are the trainers of officer candidates. Understand there may be slight variations on what these training officers and NCOs are called from one branch of service to another, it is not my intention to attempt to cover all of these details and nuances. The underlying training and training principles are similar as there is but one Department of Defense that all of the branches of the Armed Forces fall under, they are essentially separated only by their missions, for the sake of argument. The TAC officers (US Army) and training officers primarily handle the classroom instruction, while the SNCO/NCOs take care of the day-to-day management and field skills instruction. OCS is about 10 weeks (Marine Corps) and leadership is the emphasis throughout the training. Now, although there are TAC officers, make no mistake about it in the least, it is the NCO that trains. The NCOs are the ones who ensure that the TAC officers don't make fool of themselves in front of candidates. It used to be that the NCOs were tasked with mentoring the officer candidates as well as the TAC officers and would spot-check the TAC officers just like they would candidates but this has changed so that the NCO fills the role of mentor to the TAC officer instead. This is to show the candidates the dynamic role between officers and NCOs and to teach the potential officers how important the senior NCOs and Platoon Sergeants are and to rely on their experience, knowledge, and expertise in the field after OCS. I've seen it, and I know there are plenty of other enlisted soldiers and veterans who have witnessed an officer getting his "rights" read to him up and down with his behind being chewed by a SNCO (Senior/Staff Non-Commissioned Officer). And it has been proven time and again that book-smarts (officers) never outrank experience and tactical know-how (senior enlisted).

So it is the duty of the TAC officer and SNCO/NCOs to teach the candidates the required material, assess how they perform, and counsel the candidates when they fail at an objective. This is unlike basic training for enlisted soldiers (Boot Camp) where the Drill Instructor or Drill Sergeant gives all of the orders, teaches the recruit how to execute and follow orders, ensures the movement times are met, is accountable at all times for the recruit, and ensures training occurs to standards. At OCS, training schedules and expectations are what the TAC officers and NCOs provide and the responsibility of execution is left up to the officer candidates. So everything the candidates do or fail to do reflects on their leadership and it is the TAC officers and NCOs who add the stress and zero in on teachable moments when they arise. The Hon. Louis Farrakhan stated in 'The Meaning of F.O.I.' "you are to become thinking men," and this type of training would indeed produce such.

The TAC officers and NCOs use yelling as a stressor, deprive candidates of sleep, give strict time constraints after orders are given to do a task and give little to no guidance as to how the task is to be performed and completed. They do this to create an environment of high stress to acclimate the candidate to working and operating under difficult conditions. Of course, they cannot mimic the conditions of an actual combat environment but they work to get the conditions as close to it as possible which trains the candidates to focus and operate under circumstances that approach the stress levels they may experience (and then some) in combat leading soldiers when it is crucial they make competent decisions under less than ideal conditions and circumstances.

Strict time hacks are given to encourage the units to work as a team to accomplish a given task in a timely manner. These time hacks are given in such a manner that they CAN be accomplished with the right team leadership and followership working cooperatively. Decision-making is a must during OCS training, and it is better to make a wrong decision (which can be corrected during training) than no decision at all. Neglecting, or refusing, to make a decision as well as "freezing up" will get soldiers killed in combat, and so, doing so in OCS (which is a controlled environment) will most certainly get you fired. Mistakes in training can be corrected and can be learned from, mistakes in combat where lives are lost cannot.

There are other required knowledge items candidates must learn to include:

- Chain of Command
- General Orders
- Soldier's Creed (varies from one institute to another)
- 8 troop leading procedures (it used to be taught there were 6)
- 5-paragraph Operational Order (OPORD) format

and much more. The above listed are just the things one would want to be familiar with before entering training to save themselves from some of the extra exercises before meals.

Core Leader Competencies

Candidates are evaluated in all leadership positions at OCS from the Company Level (Company Commander, Executive Officer, First Sergeant) to Platoon Level (Platoon Leader, Platoon Sergeant, Squad Leader, Team Leader). Failure to achieve satisfactory ratings in any position may give the TAC officers and NCOs grounds to initiate the process to recycle a candidate or remove them from the OCS program. Such evaluations are rated on the following competencies exhibited by the candidate and how well they:

> ➤ lead others, extends influence, leads by example, communicates, creates a positive environment, prepares self, develops others, gets results, attributes, presence, intellectual capacity.

Other training includes academic and field subjects, to include:

> ➤ military history, leadership, close-order drill, land navigation, weapons, the Uniform Code of Military Justice (UCMJ), ethics in leadership, morals in leadership, basic combat skills as well as small unit leadership and infantry tactics.

In the Marine Corps, those who complete OCS training and receive their commission as 2nd Lieutenants are then sent to Quantico, Virginia for six more months of training at The Basic School (TBS). This is where newly commissioned officers learn the skills to lead Marines in combat as rifle platoon leaders. Out of all of the above-mentioned evaluations and training, ironically, officers in the United States Armed Forces are not specifically taught and trained by other commissioned officers. They are, for the most part, taught and trained by Staff non-commissioned officers (SNCOs), the very people they will be commissioned to exercise authority over (see the movie '*An Officer and A Gentleman*' as an example). The Staff NCOs and NCOs are the most experienced, professional, technically and tactically sound soldiers/Marines who are more than qualified to teach and train officers. So why, then, does the Supreme Wisdom state that the duty of the Lieutenant is to teach the private soldier; also train them? It is because officers are taught and trained to be leaders and that the best leadership is by example, always has been, always will be. And so, to be able to teach and train, expand the knowledge of and guide the growth of the private soldiers ("private" implying they belong to Allah), the officer must be and do so by EXAMPLE. Being the example is the best way to teach and train. Lead, follow, or get the hell out of the way!

Chapter 8

How to Successfully Move the Final Call Newspaper Using a Military Methodology

For years the *Final Call Newspaper* (FCN) has been referred to as the "number one program that fuels our Nation," and other such slogans. The F.O.I. have gone into the streets "pushing" this number one program and "best minister" periodical source, while avoiding, arguing in the best manner, fighting in defense, and overcoming the stigma of being mere "paperboys for Farrakhan" and other such slanderous sayings by people in the streets. Standing on street corners, enduring summer temperatures and occasionally getting a cheerful smile or kind word of encouragement from someone who purchases the FCN, the top soldiers endure and continue delivering truth as represented within the pages of the FCN. Another reality of the FCN that few like to discuss is how much debt has been accrued in the past by ordering newspapers in excess of actual customers which went in to the hundreds of thousands of dollars. Although numerous people brag on how many FCNs they were "carrying" nobody ever brags on how many FCN customers have been established and consistently maintained. And there are captains who have bragged on how many FCNs were being carried when they were in a leadership position but they never take credit for, and attention is never brought to how many FCNs were stacked in storage spaces in mosques, homes, garages, and car trunks, or how much debt there was from which the Hon. Louis Farrakhan would have to go into the No. 2 Poor Treasury to pay it off. The Most Hon. Elijah Muhammad taught us that debt makes a slave, so what logical sense does it make for the F.O.I. to go into debt over the FCN to the point that officers started using such language as "you/we have a paper-debt"?

The problem with all of this (and much more not mentioned) is that the FCN has been looked at and conducted as an individual effort, even if there were so-called "Unity Pushes" carried out, it still falls back on the individual as to what they do or fail to do. This is not how things are conducted in the military nor does it reflect any military operation or methodology. In the military, the only thing that is required of a soldier, Marine, or sailor, etc as an INDIVIDUAL is that they KEEP THEMSELVES SQUARED AWAY (regulation haircut maintained, and proper uniforms worn, shoes polished, etc.), and their weapons and gear cleaned. **Everything else is done in TEAMS, UNITS, and so forth, and TEAMWORK IS EMPHASIZED.**

In the early 90's an effort to increase door-to-door sales of the FCN and other products was attempted and proposed throughout the NOI, it was called "The Exodus Program." One of the points of this program was what was called 'Operation: 300' and its purpose was to have every F.O.I. obtain 300 customers and there was a break-down of how much monies would be earned from the sales of products. I was in San Diego at this time and a part of the weekly door-to-door pushes to obtain customers. We had contact cards that were filled out by the customer and the instructions were to turn them all in to the so-called "paper-captain". To my recollection we had reached about 500-600 contacts/customers cards turned in and then the individual who was the so-called paper-captain at that time ran off and disappeared with the monies collected as well as all of the contact cards and information. I recall Bro. Capt. Salim (may Allah be pleased with this servant) having to come before the men at F.O.I. class and explain that we were not receiving our next edition of FCNs and that we would have to sacrifice to get more for the next edition as the money was gone. Talk about de-motivation! I share this scenario because at that time I was thinking of how that whole incident could have been prevented and how it could be avoided in the future if we were more organized and tackled it in a military manner.

Years later I was teaching a military science class at Muhammad's Mosque #75 in Las Vegas, and part of the subject dealt with what is taught in the military about the 3 elements necessary to carry out any mission which are 1) assault, 2) support, and 3) security. It was at the end of this class that a brother asked "How do we use this information for what we, as F.O.I., do?" It was at this class that I realized there were men in the NOI who had never heard this information before. It was at this class that I realized how much Allah (God) truly intervenes on our behalves and in our lives as we have been talking about "our sole purpose" (mission) as F.O.I. all of this time but have no clue as to what elements are necessary to carry out our mission. And so again, the Hon. Louis Farrakhan stated he does not have "one military mosque," and it is no wonder why. So from that class I detailed a method using the above-mentioned 3 elements to put them into practice. It didn't come into fruition because not long after this class it was stated that the military science classes didn't have enough "spirit" in them. This was the case because brothers were not whooping and hollering and "bearing witness" to the information to the satisfaction of those who deemed the "spirit" was lacking. What was happening, however, was that brothers had pen and notepads in hand listening intently and taking notes from the military science information being given and so the atmosphere of the class was misinterpreted; had they stayed for the question and answer portion of the class they would have seen the enthusiasm.

Another opportunity presented itself to implement such an effort at Muhammad Mosque #15 in Atlanta, Georgia. I gave a PowerPoint presentation outlining what I called "The FCN Righteous Cause Campaign." Those armed forces veterans who were in that class remarked how they could identify the '5-paragraph order' from their military training in the presentation. At the end of this presentation the spirit and enthusiasm of the 60 plus men who were in attendance was absolutely high. And yet, once again, something occurred which prevented us from moving to the next phase of training the men on the various components and elements of said campaign. It seems as though every time we begin building and moving things in a military fashion some person with no military training or background sabotages (intentionally or unintentionally) such efforts and tries to interject themselves into the mix with a serious lack of a comprehensive knowledge of the 'how to' and the enthusiasm of the men wanes and momentum is lost and we go right back to doing things the same old ineffective way. Nevertheless, I present this 'campaign' and its details so that it may be seen, studied, questioned, implemented, given feedback on, and used successfully to boost the morale, enthusiasm, and spirit of the men as well as increase FCN sales without burdening the men. The Hon. Louis Farrakhan stated in the 'Meaning of F.O.I.':

*"So my dear and beloved brothers of the FOI, our role is a role of Saviours. What tools do you have? Knowledge, wisdom and understanding. The **Final Call** is just a tool, as are the books of the HEM. But now we must be taught how to use the tools. In the army they teach you how to shoot. In the FOI we must teach every brother how to handle himself as a soldier and how to handle the word of God as an instrument by which the people can be saved.*

So, brothers, you can see we've got a lot of training to do. And so we organize, and we go after our people in a systematic way: block by block, street by street, house by house..."

FCN Righteous Cause Campaign Synopsis:

The *Final Call Newspaper* 'Righteous Cause' Campaign is a 3-year campaign to increase the distribution and circulation of the FCN. Designed to teach the F.O.I. how to successfully execute an operation as a unit and fulfill the primary objective of military leadership which is 'mission accomplishment.'

Definition of Military Campaign:

In military science, a *military campaign* is a term applied to large scale, long duration, and significant military strategy plan incorporating a series of inter-related military operations or battles forming a distinct part of a larger conflict often called a war.

A military campaign denotes the time during which a given military force conducts combat operations in a given area (often referred to as AO, area of operation).

A military campaign is conducted with the purpose of achieving a particular desired resolution of a military conflict as its strategic goal usually within a clearly defined resource, geographic and time limited criteria.

Conduct of campaigns

Like all military operations, the military campaigns are conducted as large military projects that include the following phases:

- Initiating – clear idea of the campaign's military, political, economic, social or environmental goals
- Planning – where the General Staff define objectives, time, scope and cost of the campaign
- Executing – the coordination of forces and resources in logistic and combat operations
- Controlling – the monitoring of the progress of the campaign when compared to its baseline plan
- Concluding – acceptance or rejection of the campaign outcomes by the directing command structure

'FCN Righteous Cause Campaign'

Phase 1:

"Operation: 3,000"

This phase begins with the purchase of 150 newspaper racks (each holding 20 FCN, makes our target 3,000 papers/week) to be placed in commercial stores, we should get a discount for such a high purchase volume on the racks. Determine what that price would be and break that cost down between active FOI.

Assemble marketing/sales task force teams. Breaking the marketing task force into teams in military fashion, forming said teams and duty assignments based on **the 3 elements necessary to carry out a mission, assault, support and security**:

Assault team- this group composed of the best salesmen, is responsible for securing contracts with stores targeting the initial goal of 150 stores to place newspaper racks in. Given a target goal of 3 months (50 stores per month, dividing team up by areas and mapping said areas to identify where our market is strongest).

Support team- this group, consisting of the most reliable and consistent men, responsible for delivery of FCN to acquired store customers/clients and quality control ensuring all racks have current weekly issues and placed in highly visible area.

Security team- this group, consisting of the most reliable and trustworthy men, responsible for collecting monies from store customers/clients and keeping records and re-ordering FCN
(Have a Lieutenant over each team and assign Squad Leaders for each target area and team leaders for smaller groups working each area of responsibility)

50 stores with racks would cover 1,000 FCN, so targeting a quota of 50 stores/month gives us a projected goal of 3 months to complete mission for a total of 3,000 FCN distributed weekly. An incentive can be offered for the team that accrues the most clients and a general incentive awarded to the entire task force for reaching target goal at an earlier date.

"Operation: 2,000"

Follows same principles as first and is a 2-month operation with a goal of 2,000 FCN followed by a 1 month break after target is achieved.

"Operation: Home Stretch"

Goal is 2,000 FCN for a total of 7 months in the field. Phase 1 of campaign complete in 9 months time with a total of 7,000 FCN in circulation.

Phase 2:

"Operation: Lockbox"

This phase requires acquisition of 10 coin-operated newspaper boxes. Each box holding 50 FCN gives us 500 FCN strategically placed throughout Atlanta and surrounding counties. The responsibility of maintaining these boxes falls under the Security team. Phase 2 of campaign complete in 10 months with total of 500 FCN in circulation (totaling 7,500 with completion of Phase 1)

Phase 3:

"Operation: Grassroots"

This phase involves the door-to-door aspect of our mission to secure subscriptions, targeting 5,000 customers as a base, this is the long haul, continuous operation and can be broken into smaller manageable phases. This operation is also broken down into the elements of assault, support, and security teams in the same manner as the marketing/sales task force, and AO's (area of operation) designated by Lieutenants and the assigned areas they are in. This is a 10 month operation with a goal of acquiring 125 customers per week = 500 per month = 5,000 in 10 months) however, available men can rotate to each team as needed as not to get burnt out.

Incentives can be given for FOI who acquire the most subscriptions within X-amount of months, in addition to awarding the FOI at the end of the yearly cycle who secured the most door to door subscriptions. (Suggestion: "Fine Silk Award", as in MFM peddling silks, award could be something like giant screen tv, etc). The assault teams are responsible for the door-to-door sales and solicitation of subscriptions. The support teams are responsible for servicing said subscriptions. And the security teams are responsible for collecting monies and record keeping.

-The total FCN distributed weekly after all target objectives are met would be 12,500
-another goal of 2,500 can be set for additional newspaper racks in stores giving a total of 15,000 FCN distributed weekly from Regional HQ alone.
-the next phase of said campaign would involve targeting other cities within the region and training teams in other cities and establishing reasonable FCN target goals following the same blueprint as Regional HQ.

Other campaign details:

1) Proprietors (business owners) earn the 30 cents per issue for signing up to have FCN in stores, monies generated from door-to-door subscription sales (phase 3) will pay salary to support and security teams (who maintain records and distribution of FCN), also a commission to assault teams for securing contracts with proprietors (could be paid quarterly after x amount of subscriptions are secured

2) Two aspects of the assault team, henceforth referred to as Sales/Marketing Task Force (STF/MTF):
   a) MTF performs the reconnaissance/intel and data research and
   b) STF does the footwork and sales pitches, securing accounts, etc.

3) Support team, henceforth referred to as Distribution Task Force (DTF), keeps track of and delivers FCN to store accounts.

4) Security team, henceforth referred to as Finance Accounting & Collections Team (FACT), collects monies from store accounts and FCN re-orders plus any increases in orders.

5) All monies collected and records from teams are turned in to FCN Task Force officer in charge (OIC) who is to maintain an administrative staff to aid in accurate record keeping and collections from store sales along with subscriptions accumulated from phase 3 operations. The mosque Captain is constantly updated and made aware of said records.

6) Phase 3 teams will be broken into units based on AO's. Each team element led by an assigned team leader. Each team leader is directly under, and reports to, the squad leader(s), and the squad leader(s) reports daily to their lieutenant who makes reports to Task Force OIC on a weekly basis. Lieutenants are also responsible for logistical reports of their AO's (how much of area covered, how many subscriptions obtained, etc.).

7) Recommended that monetary collections are carried out the 1st weekend of each month for subscriptions and store accounts. Also, some type of incentive for subscribers who pay in advanced (example: $45 paid in advanced, 6 weeks plus Savior's Day edition free to customer).

Phase 4:

"Operation: Wildfire"

Mission – to duplicate organizational and strategical template throughout the southern region (and all other regions)

Phase 1 Organizational Chart

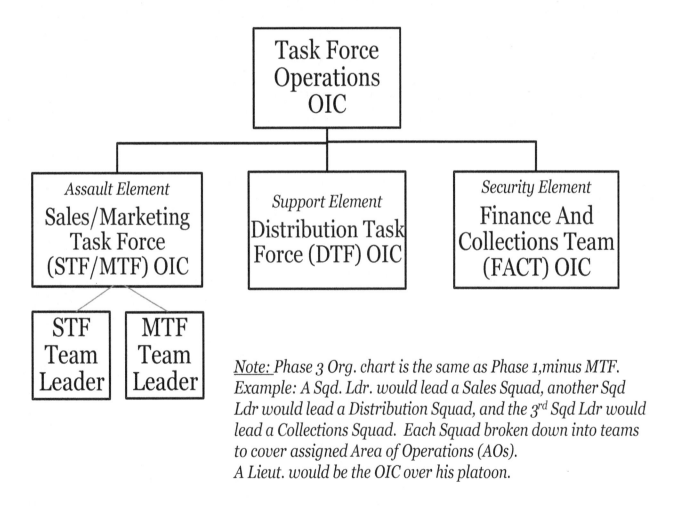

Note: Phase 3 Org. chart is the same as Phase 1, minus MTF. Example: A Sqd. Ldr. would lead a Sales Squad, another Sqd Ldr would lead a Distribution Squad, and the 3rd Sqd Ldr would lead a Collections Squad. Each Squad broken down into teams to cover assigned Area of Operations (AOs). A Lieut. would be the OIC over his platoon.

Summary:

When an individual F.O.I. accumulates FCN customers and, for example, gets 100 customers, if that individual F.O.I. becomes a casualty we don't just lose that soldier, we lose 100 people. When the FCN is tackled and organized in the above- fashioned way it forges a difficult system to overcome and no ONE casualty will cause the loss of tens of hundreds of thousands of customers gained. Structuring the distribution of the FCN in this manner takes the burden off of the individual F.O.I. and frees everyone up financially from having to come out of pocket to purchase papers individually. This freedom affords the FOI the opportunity to focus finances on other projects, increase in charity, and boosting the overall morale and spirit of the brotherhood. The 30 cents earned off of the FCN for the F.O.I. doesn't add up to much in a year's time for one individual ($30 a week for a bundle of FCN for 52 weeks = $1,560 in a year) for all of his efforts to sell FCN's. But pooling resources (as THEM taught) with 14,000 FCN in distribution as a start would yield $4,200 per week, which would be $16,800 per month, or more than $168,000 annually, not even including the 5 cents off the paper for the captains (over $36,000 per year). With this type of capital generated land could be acquired; FOI and MGT houses could be established as well as other businesses started and contributions toward education and vocation made.

Section 4

Class Outlines: Introduction to Close-Order Drill, Survival

"FOI training: when you go in close order drill, you are learning to follow simple commands. We are learning the beauty of men working together, marching together, at the command of one commander. Well, the commander-in-chief of the Nation of Islam is the Most HEM. We have no other commander. We want no other commander. All of us are stand-ins and as long as we recite His commands then we are worthy to stand in for Him. But when we begin to use His name to shield a dirty religion and then begin to impose self made commands in His name, then the FOI must be wise enough to reject such command, because it didn't come properly."

– Hon. Louis Farrakhan, *The Meaning of F.O.I.* pg 11

Chapter 9
Introduction to Close-Order Drill (Parts 1-2)

I have been a lover of military, martial arts/science, drill, uniforms and such since my youth. From marching around in a Cub-Scouts uniform (I would've been a Boy-Scout/Eagle-Scout as well but they didn't have a chapter in D.C. where I grew up), to drilling and competing in Navy JROTC during my high school days at McKinley "Tech", to drilling for countless hours in the Marine Corps. By the way, my high school JROTC was the City Inter-high Drill Champions for 10 consecutive years straight of which I was a part of for the first three, thanks to my god-father MgySgt. Charles Washington (USMC, Ret.). Our rifle drill team won countless exhibition drill competition trophies as well and we used to entertain Marines from the infamous 8th & I Barracks Marine Corps Drill Team who were impressed at our ability to perform their "mirror" routine with nearly the same precision with which they perform it. So close-order drill is not something I speak about with no background in participating in it. As the F.O.I. do not have a Standard Drill Manual, and it seems drill is not quite uniform from one region to another, I thought to add this class outline I put together several years ago. When the Hon. Louis Farrakhan led an F.O.I. class that was broadcasted via web in 2008 he stated he wanted us to do "standard drill." It is my belief, and from observation, that most men who have no military training, have demonstrated they do not know the difference between standard drill and "trick" drill when it comes to close-order drill. And so, I would like to share some facts about drill outside of what is presented in the following class outlines on 'Introduction to Close-Order Drill (Parts 1-2).

In marching, movement by a unit in an orderly manner from one place to another with the movements executed in unison with precision is what is meant by a drill. The three methods used to teach drill are 1) step-by-step, 2) by the numbers, and 3) talk-through. Cadence is the uniform step and rhythm used in marching, or the number of steps or counts per minute at which a movement is executed (a standard cadence is 120 steps per minute, or 2 steps per second). A marching step is measured from heel to heel. The historical purpose of drill is the conquest of fear, achieved through the loss of individuality and the unification of a group under obedience to orders. The "*Blue Book*" was a drill manual used by Baron Von Steuben to train the colonial army of the United States and was the predecessor of other army drill manuals. Prior to this, drill as we know it today, with the mechanical-like facing movements and such, stems from the Prussian armies. Drill is nothing more than repetitious exercise and always has been a staple of any military dating back as far as the first recorded armies. Drill was no more than practice for what would be executed on the battlefield. Before there were mechanical, non-melaninated, drill movements as was performed by the Prussians, there was rapid, flowing movements and exercises performed by the past warriors of the armies in existence prior to the making of the white man. These drill movements were the same rapid, flowing movements performed on the battlefields which made the Original Man so formidable, and made Vegetius record in '*De Re Militari*', "*We were always inferior to the African in wealth and unequal in deception and stratagem.*"

Introduction to Close-Order Drill (Part 2)

Purpose: The purpose of this period of instruction is to outline guidance in thoroughly instructing drill, the four types of commands and command voice.

Learning Objectives: Upon completion of this period of instruction the student will identify, with the aid of reference, the four types of command and general rules for drill.

Reference: Drill and Ceremonies Manual (USMC)

Body:

Points of Instructing Drill:

Training personnel in drill is an important duty. Officers and non-commissioned officers should take pride in being considered efficient drill instructors. If they know the drill regulations and how to instruct, they will gain respect and confidence of those they command.

1. Good drill instructors must:
    a. Follow regulations strictly, as an example to the personnel under instruction.
    b. Have energy, patience, and spirit.
    c. Have military neatness and bearing.
    d. Observe personnel closely, immediately correcting any mistakes noted.
2. When instructing drill movements the instructor must ensure the required information is provided:
    a. Purpose of movement.
    b. Number of counts involved in its execution.
    c. When the movement may be executed.
    d. Commands to cause the movement to be executed.
3. When instructing drill movements for unit movement the instructor must ensure the required information is provided:
    a. Purpose of movement
    b. Formation from which the movement is executed.
    c. When the movement may be executed.
    d. Commands to cause the movement to be executed.
4. When the instructor corrects movement, the individual or unit should immediately be required to repeat the movement properly.
5. Before a drill period, an instructor should thoroughly study the movements to be executed.
6. Instructors may place themselves wherever they can best control the troops, make corrections, and ensure proper performance.
7. The instructor briefly explains and demonstrates each new movement prior to its execution by the troops. The troops should take proper positions unassisted. Each position or movement must be thoroughly understood before another is attempted.
8. Drill periods should be short but frequent. Snap should be required in every movement.

Command and the Command Voice

1. There are four types of commands: preparatory commands, commands of exe-cution, combined commands, and supplementary commands.
    a. The preparatory command indicates a movement is to be made and may also indicate the direction of the movement. Example would be **"Forward"**, **"Left"**, **"Platoon"**, **"About"**, etc.
    b. The command of execution causes the desired movement to be executed. Examples would be **"MARCH", "FACE", "ATTENTION"**, etc.
    c. With the combined command, the preparatory command and the command of execution are combined. Examples would be **"AT EASE", "REST", "FALL IN"**, etc.
    d. Supplementary commands are commands that cause the component units to act individually. An example would be the commands squad leaders would give to their individual squads following the platoon commander's preparatory command, **"Column of Files From the Right",** and before the execution **"MARCH".**
2. When giving commands, commanders face their troops.
    a. For company formations or larger, when commanding marching troops from the head of a column or massed formations, commanders march backward while giving commands.
    b. When commanding a unit that is part of a larger unit, commanders turn their heads to give commands, but do not face about except when the unit is halted and the smaller units are in line. In this case, the leader faces about to give all commands except to repeat preparatory commands, for which turning the head is sufficient.
3. Commanders of platoons and larger units, when drilling as part of a still larger unit, repeat all preparatory commands or give the proper new command or warning. There are three exceptions to this.
    a. The first is that no repetition is necessary for the combined commands such as **"FALL IN", "FALL OUT", "REST",** or **"AT EASE".**
    b. The second is that no repetition of command is necessary when a unit is in mass formation.
    c. The third exception is that no repetition of command is necessary during parades and ceremonies where the commander of troops, adjutant, etc. may be clearly heard by all hands or the commander of troops and adjutant, give combined commands and subordinate unit commanders cause their units to execute the command independently.
4. If at halt, commands for movement, which involve marching at quick time in a direction other than to the direct front, such as **"Column Right, MARCH",** are not prefaced by the preparatory command, **"Forward".**
5. The only commands that use unit designations, such as "Battalion" or "Company", as preparatory commands are **"ATTENTION"** and **"HALT".** Such commands shall have no further designation added.
6. A command must be given loud enough to be heard by all members of a unit.
    a. Good posture, proper breathing, and the correct use of throat and mouth muscles help develop a commander's voice.
    b. Projecting the voice enables one to be heard at maximum range without undue strain. To project a command, commanders must focus their voices on the most distant individuals. Good exercises for voice projection are"
        1) Yawning to get the feel of the open mouth and throat.
        2) Counting and saying vowels sounds "oh" and "ah" in full, firm voice.

3) Giving commands at a uniform cadence, prolonging each syllable.

4) When practicing, stand erect, breathe properly, keep the mouth open wide, and relax the throat.

c. The diaphragm is the most important muscle in breathing. It is the large horizontal muscle that separates the chest from the abdomen. It automatically controls normal breathing, but must be developed to give commands properly. Deep breathing exercises are one good method of developing the diaphragm. Another is to take a deep breath, hold it, open the mouth, relax the throat muscles, and snap out a series of fast "hats" or "huts". Expelling short puffs of air from the lungs should make these sounds. If properly done, you can feel the stomach muscles tighten as the sounds are made.

d. The throat, mouth, and nose act as amplifiers. They give fullness to and help project the voice. In giving commands, the throat should be relaxed. The lower jaw and lips should be loose. The mouth should be open wide and the vowel sounds (a,e,i,o,u) should be prolonged. Consonants (letters other than vowels) and word endings should be curt and sharply cut off.

e. The position of attention is the proper position for giving commands. A leader's bearing will be emulated. If it is military, junior personnel will be inspired to respond to commands with snap and precision.

f. Distinct commands inspire troops. Indistinct commands confuse them. All commands can be given correctly without loss of effect or cadence. To give distinct commands, you must emphasize enunciations; make full use of the tongue, lips, and lower jaw; practice giving commands slowly, carefully, and in cadence; and then increase the rate of delivery until the proper rhythm (112 to 120 beats per minute) is reached and each syllable is distinct. Raising the hand to mouth to aid in projecting commands is not proper.

g. Inflection is the rise and fall in pitch, the tone changes of the voice.

1) Preparatory commands should be delivered with a rise and inflection in the voice. In particular those preparatory commands that cause supplemental movements should be heavily accentuated on the last syllable.

2) A command of execution is given in a sharper and higher pitch than the tone of the preparatory command's last syllable. A good command of execution has no inflection, but it must have snap. It should be delivered with sharp emphasis, ending like the crack of a whip. If properly given, the troops will react to it with snap and precision.

3) Combined commands such as **<u>FALL IN</u>** are delivered without inflection. They are given in the uniform high pitch and loudness of a command of execution.

Practice: Breathing and command voice exercises outlined in point number six.

Opportunity for Questions: None

Summary: None

As salaam alaikum

Mikaeel Shabazz Muhammad

IN THE NAME OF ALLAH, THE BENEFICENT, THE MERCIFUL

Introduction to Close-Order Drill (Part 1)

Purpose: The purpose of this period of instruction is to review the purpose of close-order drill, the purpose of formations, and define standard terms used in close-order drill.

Learning Objectives: Upon completion of this period of instruction the student will identify, with the aid of reference, the purpose of close-order drill and standard terms used in close-order drill.

Reference: Drill and Ceremonies Manual (USMC)

Body: def.   **drill** – [<Du drillen, to bore] **2.** a) systematic military or physical training

b) the method of practice of teaching by repeated exercises

order – [< L ordo, straight row] **1.** social position **2.** a state of peace; orderly conduct **3.** arrangement of things or events; series **4.** a definite plan; system **5.** a military, monastic, or social brotherhood **6.** a condition in which everything is in its place and working properly **7.** condition in general {in good order] **8.** an authoritative command, instruction, etc. **9.** a class; kind **10.** an established method, as of conduct in meetings, etc.

- vt. 1. to put or keep (things) in order; arrange **2.** to command **3.** to request (something to be supplied)

Purpose of Drill – Commanders use drill to:

a.   Move units from one place to another in a standard, orderly manner,
b.   Provide simple formations from which combat formations may be readily assumed.
c.   Teach discipline by instilling habits of precision and automatic response to orders.
d.   Increase the confidence of junior officers and non-commissioned officers through the exercise of command, by the giving of proper commands, and by the control of drilling troops.

Purpose of Formations:

a.   To build unit cohesion and esprit de corps by recognizing soldiers during awards and promotion ceremonies.
b.   To maintain continuous accountability and control of personnel.
c.   To provide frequent opportunities to observe the appearance and readi-ness of the uniforms and equipment of the individual soldier.
d.   To keep the individual soldier informed by providing the means to pass the word.

e. To develop command presence in unit leaders.
f. To instill and maintain high standards of military bearing and appearance in units and in the individual soldier.
g. To add color and dignity to the daily routine by reinforcing the traditions of excellence associated with close order drill.

Standard terms and their definitions.

1. **Alignment** - The dressing of several elements on a straight line.
2. **Assembly Area** - A designated location for forming units of platoon size or larger for a parade, review or ceremony.
3. **Arms** - A term used to refer to any weapon.
4. **Base** - The element on which a movement is regulated.
5. **Cadence** - A rhythmic rate of march at a uniform step.
6. **Center** - The middle element of a formation with an odd number of elements or the left center of a formation with an even number of elements.
7. **Ceremony** - A formal military formation designated to observe a specific occasion.
8. **Column** - A formation in which elements are placed one behind the other. A section or platoon is in column when members of each squad are one behind the other with the squads abreast of each other.
9. **Depth** - The space from head to rear of an element or formation. The depth of an individual is considered to be 12 inches.
10. **Distance** - The space between elements in the direction of depth. Between individuals, the space between your chest and the person to your front. Between vehicles, the space between the front end of a vehicle and the rear of the vehicle to its front. Between troops in formation (either on foot, mounted, or in vehicles), the space from the front of the rear unit to the rear of the unit in front. Platoon commanders, guides, and others whose positions in a formation are 40 inches from a rank are, themselves, considered a rank. Otherwise, commanders and those with them are not considered in measuring distance between units. The color guard is not considered in measuring distance between subdivisions of the unit with which it is posted. In troop formations, the distance between ranks is 40 inches.
11. **Double Time** - Cadence at 180 steps (36 inches in length) per minute.
12. **Element** - An individual, squad, section, platoon, company, or other unit that is part of a larger unit.
13. **Extended Mass Formation** - The formation of a company or larger unit in which major elements are in column at close or normal interval and abreast at a specified interval greater than normal interval.
14. **File** - A single column of troops or vehicles one behind the other.
15. **Flank** - The right or left extremity of a unit, either in line or in column. The element on the extreme right or left of the line. A direction at a right angle to the direction an element or a formation is facing.
16. **Formation** - Arrangement of elements of a unit in line, in column, or in any other prescribed manner.
17. **Front** - The space occupied by an element or a formation, measured from one flank to the other. The front of an individual is considered to be 22 inches.

18. **Guide** - The individual (base) upon whom a formation, or other elements thereof, regulates its march. To guide; to regulate interval, direction, or alignment; to regulate cadence on a base file (right, left, center).
19. **Head** - The leading element of a column.
20. **Interval** - The lateral space between elements on the same line. Interval is measured between individuals from shoulder to shoulder. It is measured between elements other than individuals and between formations from flank to flank. Unit commanders and those with them are not considered in measuring interval between elements of the unit. Normal interval between individuals is one arm's length. Close interval is the horizontal distance between shoulder and elbow when the left hand is placed on the left hip.
21. **Left (Right)** - Extreme left (right) element or edge of a body of troops.
22. **Line** - A formation in which the elements are side by side or abreast of each other. A section or platoon is in line when its squads are in line and one behind the other.
23. **Line of March** - The line on which individuals or units are to march on.
24. **Line of Troops** - The line on which troops are to form when in formation.
25. **Mass Formation** - The formation of a company or larger unit in which the major elements are in column at close interval and abreast at close interval.
26. **Pace** - The length of a full step in quick time, 30 inches.
27. **Parade** - A parade is a ceremony that involves the movement of marching units.
28. **Point of Rest** - The point toward which all elements of a unit establish their dress or alignment.
29. **Quick Time** - Cadence at 112 to 120 steps (12, 15, or 30 inches in length) per minute. It is normal cadence for drills and ceremonies.
30. **Rank** - A line of troops or vehicles placed side by side.
31. **Review** - A review is a type of ceremony that omits certain elements found in a parade, but includes an inspection (trooping the line) not found in a parade.
32. **Rigged** - This term refers to the condition when uniforms and equipment are properly fitted out in the manner for which they were intended for use. A soldier is rigged when wearing the prescribed uniform and equipment.
33. **Slow Time** - Cadence at 60 steps per minute. Used for funerals only.
34. **Snap** – In commands or signals, the quality that inspires immediate response. In drill the immediate and smart execution of a movement.
35. **Step** - The distance from heel to heel between the feet of a marching individual. The half step and back step are 15 inches. The right and left steps are 12 inches. The steps in quick and double time are 30 and 36 inches.
36. **Strong Grip** - The strong grip is when the thumb is wrapped around the front of the staff with the fingers wrapped to the rear.
37. **Unit Leader** - Is the individual who is drilling the unit. This can be any indivi-dual who is conducting drill or can be those assigned a specific billet such as squad leader, platoon sergeant, platoon commander, etc.
38. **"V" Grip** - The "V" grip is with the staff placed in the "V" formed by the thumbs and forefinger with the fingers extended and joined.

Practice: None

Opportunity for Questions: None

Summary: None

As salaam alaikum

Bro. Mikaeel Shabazz Muhammad

Chapter 10
Survival Training (1-2)

The following class outlines were comprised of information as presented in three survival training manuals, *How To Survive On Land And Sea* by F. Craighead and J. Craighead, the US *Army Survival Manual – FM* (Field Manual) 21-76, and the *US Air Force Search and Rescue Survival Training* – AF Reg. 64-4. There are more survival training manuals available, my intention was to take the essential information provided in each and condense it into a few class outlines/handouts to be used for F.O.I. class. So as much of the information was repeated or similar from each of the manuals, the information presented in the class outlines represents invaluable information that can be used as a quick reference guide of what to consider and be prepared for in a survival situation. There was more information I intended to cover and two more outlines on survival that I was preparing so by no means is the information complete, but it is a start.

Years ago, in almost every mosque, there would be a chalkboard with the flag representing the United States and the Flag of Islam, as well as a cross on the side of the U.S. flag along with the words "Which one will survive the War of Armageddon?" The word survive is from the Latin word *supervivere* (super + *vivere* to live) and as an intransitive verb means 1) to remain alive or in existence, 2) to continue to function or prosper. As a transitive verb, survive means 1) to remain alive after the death of, 2) to continue to exist or live after, and 3) to continue to function or prosper despite: withstand. In all of the survival training manuals and courses you could possible read and take there are 3 things that I consider to be the core elements and fundamentals of them all, and that is:

1) Willpower (reinforced by mental and physical conditioning)
2) Preparation (which includes planning, training, and study)
3) Adaptability

Survival is not just about stocking up on canned and dry goods or other materials. You could have stockpiles of both and still succumb to death from lacking the willpower or mental fortitude to overcome (or adapt to) whatever tragic situation or catastrophe encountered. Preparation is always the key, and there is nothing like training and conditioning, along with study to prepare. That is what military training is about.

Military Science

Survival Training (Part 1): Willpower, Mental Strength and Physical Preparation

Purpose: The purpose of this instruction is to introduce survival and training methods as taught and utilized by soldiers of the armed forces.

Learning Objectives: Upon completion of this period of instruction the student will, with the aid of reference, identify threats to successful survival, identify 8 points to help as a person in a survival situation struggles to exert command over a life-threatening situation and identify the three elementary needs of a survivor.

References: How To Survive On Land And Sea – F. Craighead and J. Craighead, US Army Survival Manual – FM 21-76, US Air Force Search and Rescue Survival Training – AF Reg. 64-4

Body:

SECTION A

Psychological Aspects of Survival – Emotional Reactions, Stresses, Pain, Thirst and Dehydration, Cold and Heat, Hunger, Frustration, Fatigue, Sleep Deprivation, Isolation, Insecurity, Loss of Self-Esteem, Loss of Self-Determination, Depression

Survival depends largely upon preparedness and resourcefulness. There are emotional aspects associated with survival that must be completely understood just as survival conditions and equipment are understood. An important factor bearing on success or failure in a survival episode is the individual's psychological state. Maintaining a balanced, positive/optimistic psychological state or outlook on a given situation depends on the individual's ability to cope with numerous factors. Some to consider include:

1) Understanding how various physiological and emotional signs, feelings and expressions affect one's bodily needs and mental attitude.
2) Managing physical and emotional reactions to stressful situations.
3) Knowing individual psychological and physical tolerance limits.
4) Exerting a positive influence on companions.

Everyone is endowed with biological mechanisms that aid in adapting to stress. For example, the bodily changes that result from fear and anger tend to increase alertness and provide an adrenaline rush stimulating the "flight/fight" response. However, these and other mechanisms can hinder a person under survival conditions. For instance, a survivor in a raft at sea could cast aside rationale and reasoning and drink seawater to quench a thirst; or, evaders in enemy territory, driven by hunger pangs, could expose themselves to capture while searching for food. These examples illustrate how "normal" reactions to stress could create problems for a survivor.

Two of the gravest threats to successful survival are concessions to comfort and apathy. Both threats represent attitudes which must be avoided. **To survive, a person must focus planning and effort on fundamental needs.**

Survivors must value life more than comfort, and be willing to tolerate heat, hunger, dirt, itching, pain and any other discomfort. Recognizing discomfort is temporary will help survivors concentrate on effective action.

As the will to keep trying lessens, drowsiness, mental numbness, and indifference will result in apathy. This apathy usually builds up slowly, but ultimately takes over and leaves a survivor helpless. Physical factors can contribute to apathy. Exhaustion due to prolonged exposure to the elements, loss of body fluids (dehydration), fatigue, weakness, or injury are all conditions which can contribute to apathy. Proper planning and sound decisions can help a survivor avoid these conditions. Lastly, survivors must watch for signs of apathy in companions and help prevent it. The first signs are resignation, quietness, lack of communication, loss of appetite, and withdrawal from the group. Preventive measures could include maintaining group morale by planning, activity, and getting the organized participation of all members.

In survival situations, many common stresses cause reactions which can be recognized and dealt with appropriately. A survivor must understand stresses and reactions often occur at the same time. Although survivors will face many stresses, the following common stresses will occur in virtually all survival episodes: pain, thirst, cold and heat, hunger, frustration, fatigue, sleep deprivation, isolation, insecurity, loss of self-esteem, loss of self determination, and depression.

Pain: Like fever, pain is a warning signal calling attention to an injury or damage to some part of the body. Pain is discomforting but is not, in itself, harmful or dangerous. Pain can be controlled, and in an extremely grave situation, survival must take priority over giving in to pain. Its biological function is to protect an injured part by warning the individual to rest it to avoid using it. In a survival situation, the normal pain warnings may have to be ignored in order to meet more critical needs. Concentration and intense effort can actually stop or reduce feelings of pain. Sometimes this concentration may be all that is needed to survive.

The following facts about pain must be understood by a survivor:

1) Despite pain, a survivor can move in order to live.
2) Pain can be reduced by: a) understanding its source and nature, b) recognizing pain as a discomfort to be tolerated, c) concentrating on necessities like thinking, planning, and keeping busy, d) developing confidence and self respect.

When personal goals of maintaining life, honor, and overcoming the situation are valued highly enough, a survivor can tolerate almost anything.

Thirst and Dehydration: The lack of water and its accompanying problems of thirst and dehydration are among the most critical problems facing survivors. Thirst can be tolerated if the will to carry on, supported by calm, purposeful activity, is strong. Although thirst indicates the body's need for water, it does not indicate how much water is needed. Drinking only enough water to satisfy thirst does not prevent the possibility of slowly dehydrating. Prevention of thirst and the more debilitating dehydration is possible if survivors drink plenty of water any time it is available, and especially when eating.

When the body's water balance is not maintained, thirst and discomfort result. Ultimately, a water imbalance will result in dehydration. The need for water may be increased if the person has a fever, is fearful, perspires unnecessarily, or rations water rather than sweat. Dehydration decreases the body's efficiency or ability to function. Minor degrees of dehydration may not noticeably affect a survivor's performance, but as it becomes more severe, body functioning will become increasingly impaired. Slight dehydration and thirst can also cause irrational behavior. While prevention is the best way to avoid dehydration, virtually any degree of dehydration is reversible simply by drinking water.

Cold and Heat: The average normal body temperature for a person is 98.6 degrees Fahrenheit. Victims have survived a body temperature as low as 20 degrees below normal, but consciousness is clouded and thinking numbed at a much smaller drop. An increase of 6 to 8 degrees above normal for any prolonged period may prove fatal. Any deviation from normal temperature, even by as little as 1 or 2 degrees, reduces efficiency.

Cold is a serious stress since even in mild degrees it lowers efficiency. Extreme cold numbs the mind and dulls the will to do anything except get warm again. Cold numbs the body by lowering the flow of blood to the extremities, and results in sleepiness. Survivors have endured prolonged cold and dampness through exercise, proper hygiene procedures, shelter, and food. Wearing proper clothing and having the proper climatic survival equipment when traversing through cold weather areas are essential to enhance survivability.

Just as "numbness" is the principal symptom of cold, "weakness" is the principle symptom of heat. Most people can adjust to high temperatures. It my take from two days to a week before circulation, breathing, heart action, and sweat glands are all adjusted to a hot climate. Heat stress also accentuates dehydration, which was discussed earlier. In addition to the problem of water, there are many other sources of discomfort and impaired efficiency which are directly attributable to heat or to the environmental conditions in hot climates. Extreme temperature changes, from extremely hot days to very cold nights, are experienced in desert and plains areas. Proper use of clothing and shelters can decrease the adverse effects of such extremes. Bright sun has a tremendous effect on eyes and exposed skin. Direct sunlight or rays reflecting off the terrain require dark glasses or improvised eye protectors. Protective clothing is important. Wind can constitute an additional discomfort and difficulty in desert areas when it carries particles of sand and dirt. Protection against sand and dirt can be provided by tying a cloth around the head after cutting slits for vision.

Acute fear has been experienced among survivors in sandstorms and snowstorms. This fear results from both the terrific impact of the storm itself and its obliteration of landmarks showing direction of travel. Finding or improving shelter for protection from the storm itself is important. Loss of moisture, drying of the mouth and mucous membranes, and accelerated dehydration can be caused by breathing through the mouth and talking. Survivors must learn to keep their mouth shut in desert winds as well as in cold weather.

Mirages and illusions of many kinds are common in desert areas. These illusions not only distort visual perception but sometimes account for serious accidents. In the desert, distances are usually greater than they appear and, under certain conditions, mirages obstruct accurate vision. Inverted reflections are a common occurrence.

Hunger: A considerable amount of edible material (which survivors may not initially regard as food) may be available under survival conditions. Hunger and semi-starvation are more commonly experienced among survivors than thirst and dehydration. Research has revealed no evidence of permanent damage nor any decrease in mental efficiency from short periods of total fasting. Frequently, in the excitement of some survival, evasion, and escape episodes, hunger is forgotten. Survivors have gone for considerable lengths of time without food or awareness of hunger pains. An early effort should be made to procure and consume food to reduce the stresses brought on by food deprivation. If food deprivation is complete and only water is ingested, the pangs of hunger disappear in a few days, but even then the mood changes of depression and irritability occur. The individual tendency is still to search for food to prevent starvation and such efforts might continue as long as strength and self-control permit. When the food supply is limited, even strong friendships are threatened.

Controlling hunger during survival episodes is relatively easy if the survivor can adjust to discomfort and adapt to primitive conditions.

Frustration: Frustration occurs when one's efforts are stopped, either by obstacles blocking progress toward a goal or by not having a realistic goal. It can occur if the feeling of self-worth or self-respect is lot. A wide range of obstacles, both environmental and internal, can lead to frustration. Frustrating conditions often create anger, accompanied by a tendency to attack and remove the obstacles to goals. Frustration must be controlled by channeling energies into a positive and worthwhile obtainable goal. The survivor should complete the easier tasks before attempting more challenging ones. This will not only instill self-confidence, but also relive frustration.

Fatigue: In a survival episode, a survivor must continually cope with fatigue and avoid the accompanying strain and loss of efficiency. A survivor must be aware of the dangers of over-exertion. In many cases, a survivor may already be experiencing strain and reduced efficiency as a result of other stresses such as heat or cold, dehydration, hunger, or fear. A survivor must judge capacity to walk, carry, lift, or do necessary work, and plan and act accordingly. During an emergency, considerable exertion may be necessary to cope with the situation. If an individual understands fatigue and the attitudes and feelings generated by various kinds of effort, that individual should be able to call on available reserves of energy when they are needed.

A survivor must avoid complete exhaustion which may lead to physical and psychological changes. A survivor should be able to distinguish between exhaustion and being uncomfortably tired. Although a person should avoid working to complete exhaustion, in emergencies certain tasks must be done in spite of fatigue. Rest is a basic factor for recovery from fatigue and is also important in resisting further fatigue. It is essential that the rest (following fatiguing effort) be sufficient to permit complete recovery; otherwise, the residual fatigue will accumulate and require longer periods of rest to recover from subsequent effort. During the early stages of fatigue proper rest provides a rapid recovery. This is true of muscular fatigue as well as mental fatigue. Sleep is the most complete form of rest available and is basic to recovery from fatigue. Fatigue can be reduced by working "smarter". This is done by adjusting the pace of the effort. Balance the load, the rate, and the time period. And adjust the technique of work. Economy of effort is important.

Sleep Deprivation: The effects of sleep loss are closely related to those of fatigue. Sleeping at unaccustomed times, sleeping under strange circumstances, or missing part or the entire accustomed amount of sleep will cause a person to react with feelings of weariness, irritability, emotional tension, and some loss of efficiency. Strong motivation is one of the principal factors in helping to compensate for the impairing effects of sleep loss. Superior mental and physical conditioning, opportunities to rest, food and water, help in enduring sleep deprivation.

Isolation: Loneliness, helplessness, and despair, which are experienced by survivors when they are isolated, are among the most severe survival stresses. Isolation can be controlled and overcome by knowledge, understanding, deliberate countermeasures, and a determined will to resist it.

Insecurity: Insecurity is the survivor's feeling of helplessness or inadequacy resulting from varied stresses and anxieties. These anxieties may be caused by uncertainty regarding individual goals, abilities, and the future in a survival situation. Feelings of insecurity may have widely different effects on the survivor's behavior. A survivor should establish challenging but attainable goals. The better a survivor feels about individual abilities to achieve goals and adequately meet personal needs, the less insecure the survivor will feel.

Loss of Self-Esteem: Self-esteem is the state or quality of having personal self-respect and pride. Lack of (or loss of) self-esteem in a survivor may bring on depression and a change in perspective and goals. A loss of self-esteem may occur in individuals in captivity. Humiliation and other factors brought on by the captor may cause them to doubt their own worth. Humiliation comes from the feeling of losing pride or self-respect by being disgraced or dishonored, and is associated with the loss of self-esteem. Survivors should try to maintain proper perspective about both the situation and themselves.

Loss of Self-Determination: A self-determined person is relatively free from external controls or influences over his or her actions. In everyday society, these "controls and influences" are the laws and customs of our society and of the self-imposed elements of our personalities. In a survival situation, the "controls and influences" can be very different. Survivors may feel as if events, circumstances, and (in some cases) other people, are in control of the situation. A lack of self-determination is more perceived than actual. Survivors must decide how unpleasant factors will be allowed to affect their mental state. They must have the self-confidence, fostered by experience and training, to live with their feelings and decisions, and to accept responsibility for both the way they feel and how they let those feelings affect them.

Depression: As a survivor, depression is the biggest psychological problem that has to be conquered. It should be acknowledged that everyone has mental "highs" and "lows". People experiencing long periods of sadness or other negative feelings are suffering from depression. A normal mood associated with the sadness, grief, disappointment, or loneliness that everyone experiences at times is also described as depression. Most of the emotional changes in mood are temporary and do not become chronic. Depressed survivors may feel fearful, guilty, or helpless. They may lose interest in the basic needs of life. Many cases of depression also involve pain, fatigue, loss of appetite, or other physical ailments. Some depressed survivors try to injure or kill themselves. The main reason depression is a most difficult problem is that it can affect a wide range of psychological responses. Depression usually begins after a survivor has met the basic needs for sustaining life, such as water, shelter, and food. Once the survivor's basic needs are met, there is often too much time for that person to dwell on the past, the present predicament, and on future problems. The survivor must be aware of the necessity to keep the mind and body active to eliminate the feeling of depression.

The Will to Survive – Overcoming Stress, Crisis Period, Coping, Attitude, Optimism/Faith

The *will to survive* is defined as the desire to live despite seemingly insurmountable mental and (or) physical obstacles. Tools and training are not enough without a will to survive. Many survival case histories show that stubborn, strong willpower can conquer many obstacles. In fact, the records prove that "will" alone has been the deciding factor in many survival cases. A single-minded survivor with a powerful *will to survive* can overcome most hardships.

Overcoming Stress: The mind has the ability to overcome stress and hardship even in situations where there appears to be little chance of a person surviving. When there appears to be no escape from the situation, the "will" enables a person to begin to win "the battle of the mind". This mental attitude can bridge the gap between the crisis period and the coping period.

<u>Crisis Period</u>:   This is the point at which the person realizes the gravity of the situation and understands that the problem will not go away. At this stage, what is needed is action. Not being ready to face such a challenge may cause a person to experience shock.

Preparation through knowledge and training may enable most people to recover control of their faculties. Shock during a normal crisis is normally a response to being overcome with anxiety. Thinking will be disorganized. At this stage, direction will be required because the individual is being controlled by the environment. If the situation continues to control the individual or group, the response may be panic, behavior may be irrational, and judgment is impaired. In a lone-survivor episode, the individual must gain control of the situation and respond constructively. Survivors must evaluate the situation and develop a plan of action. During the evaluation, the survivor must determine the most critical needs to improve survivability.

<u>The Coping Period</u>:   This period begins after the survivor recognizes the gravity of the situation and resolves to endure it rather than succumb. The survivor must tolerate the effects of physical and emotional stresses.   These stresses can cause anxiety, which becomes the greatest obstacle to self-control and solving problems. Coping with the situation requires considerable internal control. Survivors must often subdue urges to do things that are counterproductive and dangerous. Those who fail to think constructively may panic. This could begin a series of mistakes that result in further exhaustion, injury, and sometimes death. Death comes not from hunger pains but from the inability to manage or control emotions and thought processes.

<u>Attitude</u>:   The most important element of the *will to survive* is the survivor's attitude. Almost anything is possible with the proper attitude. The desire to live is sometimes based on the feelings toward another person and (or) thing. Love and hatred are two emotional extremes that have moved people to do exceptional things physically and mentally. The lack of a will to survive can sometimes be identified by the individual's motivation to meet essential survival needs, emotional control resulting in reckless, panic-like behavior, and self-esteem. It is essential to strengthen the will to survive during an emergency. The first step being to avoid "flying off the handle" or the tendency to panic. Sit down, relax, and analyze the situation rationally. Once thoughts are collected and thinking is clear, the next step is to make decisions. Failure to decide on a course of actions is actually a decision for inaction. This lack of decision-making may even result in death. Decisiveness must be tempered with flexibility and planning for unforeseen circumstances. Tolerance is another topic of concern. A survivor will have to deal with many physical and psychological discomforts, such as unfamiliar animals, insects, loneliness, and depression. Survivors must face and overcome fears to strengthen the will to survive. These fears may be founded or unfounded, be generated by the survivor's uncertainty or lack of confidence. Despite the source of the fear, survivors must recognize fear and make a conscious effort to overcome it.

<u>Optimism/Faith:</u> One of a survivor's key assets is optimism-hope and faith. Survivors must maintain a positive, optimistic outlook on their circumstances and how well they are doing. Prayer or meditation can be helpful. How a survivor maintains optimism is not so important as its use, as prayer or meditation without proper planning and action are fruitless.

SECTION B

Preparation – Mental Strength and Physical Readiness, Realistic Assessment of Abilities, Medications and Other Requirements, Equipment Preparation

The desire to live and a healthy frame of mind to fulfill that desire may be the critical factors determining whether you live or die. Individuals in a survival situation must battle panic and hysteria as well as loneliness and boredom.

Panic is the number-one-enemy. All too often, avoidable tragedy results from the actions of one who succumbs to this killer. Panic is simply unreasoning and uncontrollable fear...A certain amount of fear is good in that its physical changes – elevated pulse, increased respiration, and tensed muscles – coupled with an increased tolerance for pain equip animals and humans alike with a powerful will to survive. But extreme fear or panic is self-defeating. You must allow your greatest asset, your ability to think logically, to come to the fore.

If you are to survive, you must calm yourself and carefully assess the situation. Determine the necessary actions and then execute them in a logical sequence. Although you should at all times be aware of any opportunities for rescue or escape, you should prepare yourself for a long period of just staying alive. – from How to Survive on Land and Sea (F. Craighead, Jr. and J. Craighead)

In addition to the valid points made by the authors in the above excerpt, they list the following eight points to help as a person in a survival situation struggles to exert command over a life-threatening situation:

(1) Study your plight – optimistically.
(2) Organize your approach to the challenge by recalling what you know of survival techniques. Set priorities.
(3) Decide upon definite goals such as setting a course, deploying survival gear, procuring water and food, or sending radio signals.
(4) Inventory your water and food and make arrangements to supplement your cache before you actually need to. Save every piece of equipment you can, as you may find a use for it.
(5) Control your fear by steadily replacing the unknown with the known. Make use of your heightened powers brought on by the biological response to fear but don't give in to panic.
(6) Hope for rescue or escape, but prepare mentally and physically for further hazards.
(7) Stay busy, to keep fear and loneliness at bay.
(8) Refuse to give in for any momentary desire for relief, and realize that your body will respond to your demands and to the rigors of your predicament. Be unyielding.

According to the authors, "Second only to fortitude – and a close second at that – is your degree of physical readiness. Common sense dictates that the individual in good general physical condition is much more likely to survive than someone who is not. Maintaining a regular program of physical fitness will give you a head start toward surviving an emergency in a hostile environment."

Worse than being in poor physical condition in a survival situation is not realizing that you are out of shape and unfit. A realistic assessment of your physical abilities must be made. Relying on past physical athletic achievements from your high school or college football and basketball days is unrealistic, especially if it has been more than a couple of years that have passed since those last achievements.

Do not try to do more than you are capable of doing and after a realistic assessment of your physical capabilities restrict your activities accordingly. Your survival expectancy is not determined by this assessment, the purpose is to plan your activities and be knowledgeable of what you are capable of doing. This will help prevent you from succumbing unnecessarily to the elements. The old adage of "preparation is key" is true and valid with regards to being in the best physical condition possible and knowing your physical limitations.

Being prepared in general terms isn't enough if you as an individual have your own special medical requirements due to personal handicaps that may present a problem in a survival situation. Persons who are diabetic, have hypertension and other such ailments which require medication may want to stock up on necessary prescriptions of said medication and also be mindful that such ailments and medicinal requirements may present even more of a problem should travel become necessary. The ideal course would be to follow the guidelines as taught by the Most Honorable Elijah Muhammad in How to Eat to Live books 1 & 2 which, if followed, would aid a person in ridding the body of such ailments. Also, becoming knowledgeable of medicinal plants and herbs and learning to treat one's self with what is available in the wilderness is beneficial, as another old wise saying "let your food be your medicine and your medicine be your food" is applicable too.

<u>Equipment Preparation</u>

You would want to prepare a supply kit that would help you respond to basic needs relevant to the survival situation you believe you are most likely to experience. In planning your survival kit you face such questions as: What situation am I most likely to confront? What type of equipment should I have? For how long might I have to survive on my own? How often should I inspect my gear? How can the gear be stored without it taking over all the space I have? How do I school myself ahead of time in the use of emergency equipment? What should be included and what can be safely excluded?

Imagine yourself in the survival context you are most likely to encounter and judge for yourself what equipment you will need. The recommendations of salespeople and books are helpful, but don't feel like you must conform religiously to them.

The required gear for a vehicle (ie, car, boat, etc) is a good place to start as nearly all vehicles are equipped in some way to meet various emergencies. Consult books or magazines whose express purpose is to evaluate the many survival products on the market. Many government agencies and private concerns provide comprehensive lists of both required and suggested emergency equipment for various vehicles. Many of the items can be accommodated in a backpack. High on all lists are first aid kits and signaling flares (however in hostile environments, signal flares present a risk of signaling and alerting the wrong persons to your position). Other items useful in virtually any survival situation are such things as flashlight, matches or flint and steel, and a strong knife. It is also good to have some canned water, hard candy, dried fruit, and boullion cubes handy.

Much of the equipment people use in the wilderness can double as survival gear, if the need arises. Some of the supplies that one might carry are not consumable, such as a knife, signal mirror, etc. Some are consumable but not on a daily basis, such as first aid items, flares, flashlight batteries. Some items such as waterproof matches, water purification tablets, and most personal medicines are consumable but can be purchased in quantity very cheaply and stored in a small space. The real decision which must be made is how much canned or bottled water to carry and how much and what kind of food. Most people carry neither of these and hope that they are either not needed or that nature will provide. Although the possibility exists that you may have to survive in the wilderness or at sea longer that you have prepared for, there is a point of diminishing returns in the preparation for any emergency.

It is not enough to merely install a survival package in some out-of-the-way place in your car, boat, airplane, or other vehicle. You must regularly inspect your gear to determine whether you have the gear you need, in the proper quantity, and in satisfactory condition.

Ask yourself the following questions: Is gear available for potential survival needs? Do you have a checklist of emergency equipment required for your type of traveling? Is there anything special about the intended trip that will warrant a change in the normal survival package, such as a prolonged over-water flight? Are you dressed properly? Are there sufficient quantities of each item in the survival package? Does the first aid kit or road flare bundle require replenishing? Will a special trip require additional food stuffs? Is the emergency equipment equal to the potential task? Is the quality of the gear good? If the various items were needed in an emergency would they operate correctly? Is the equipment in good condition? Has the emergency package been sitting in the trunk of the car for several years without being inspected? Have any pests gotten into the powdered food? Do any of the water containers show signs of contamination? Are the batteries in various items still good? Regular inspection should reassure you regarding the type, quality, quantity, and condition of your survival equipment and supplies.

It is pointless to have the correct equipment, in good repair, and in sufficient quantity if you don't know how to use it. Precious minutes may be lost because you are fumbling through the directions to learn how to administer first aid or operate a flare. It is often well worth the slight additional expense to actually practice with the equipment. Most equipment can be used and replaced. A first aid course is strongly recommended for all people whether they travel or not. In addition, actual outdoors experience in constructing a shelter would be useful. Prepare some meals with powdered food at home to see what it tastes like. Try cutting wood with a wire saw, setting up a solar or vegetable still, purifying water, or making a snare with branches and vines. Become familiar with the equipment you carry and know how to use it properly. Periodically practice with the equipment and review its literature.

Survival Planning – Importance of Planning, Survivor's Needs, Survival Kit, Selection of Survival Kit Items

Survival planning is nothing more than realizing that something could happen that would put you in a survival situation and, with that realization, taking steps to increase your chances of survival. In other words, survival planning is **being prepared**.

Being prepared means you have survival items with you, and know how to use them. You can train, practice, and prepare to meet any survival challenge. The details in survival planning may seem of little importance, however, they can become quite significant if a survival situation arises. Imagine how your chances of success in evading an enemy would decrease if you were wearing new or improperly fitted boots. A person who normally is not required to walk long distances will tend to overlook the importance of proper footgear. A small detail that is extremely important when working in an arid area is conserving water. You must make maximum use of the available water. Another small detail is preventive medicine. Have your teeth checked, a tooth problem in a survival situation will greatly reduce your ability to cope with other problems you may face.

Survivor's needs

Three elementary needs of a survivor in any situation which are categorized as the integral components of maintaining life are: personal protection, sustenance, and health.

The survivor's primary defenses against the effects of the environment are clothing, equipment, shelter, and fire. Additionally, clothing, equipment, and shelter are the primary defenses against some of the effects of induced conditions.

The need for adequate clothing and its proper care and use cannot be overemphasized. The human body's tolerance for temperature extremes is very limited. However, its ability to regulate heating and cooling is extraordinary. The availability of clothing and its proper use is extremely important to a survivor in using these abilities of the body. Clothing also provides excellent protection against the external effects of alpha and beta radiation, and may serve as a shield against the external effects of some chemical or biological agents. The survivor's need for shelter is twofold – as a place to rest and for protection from the effects of the environmental and (or) induced conditions (nuclear, biological or chemical). The duration of the survival episode will have some effect on shelter choice. In areas that are warm and dry, the survivor's need is easily satisfied using natural resting places. In cold climates, the criticality of shelter can be measured in minutes, and rest is of little immediate concern. Similarly, in areas of residual radiation, the criticality of shelter may also be measured in minutes.

Fire serves as many survivor needs: purifying water, cooking and preserving food, signaling, and providing a source of heat to warm the body and dry clothing. Survivors need food and water to maintain normal body functions and to provide strength, energy, and endurance to overcome the physical stresses of survival (review and study How to Eat to Live books 1&2 by THEM).

Survival Kit

When assembling a general survival kit for land or sea, refer to the items listed below. In addition, consider special protective clothing and footwear and other special tools and equipment recommended for specific geographical areas. Items marked with an asterisk (*) are considered to be the "bare bones" of a survival kit. Also included in all survival kits should be a survival manual.

First Aid Kit

* (1) Sterile gauze dressings (sealed in plastic bag)

* (2) Bandages 2"x2"

* (3) Compress-type bandages 3" wide roll/s

* (4) Muslin bandage 37"x37"x52"

* (5) Adhesive tape (roll/s)

* (6) Band-Aids, 25 each large

* (7) Alcohol (in plastic container)

  (8) Sunburn prevention ointment

* (9) Aspirin (the herb Wood Betony is a natural aspirin)

 (10) Local antiseptic solution (such as benzalkonium chloride)

 (11) Snake bite kit

(12) Baking soda

(13) Insect repellant (Skin-So-Soft and alcohol work well)

(14) Aromatic ampules (1/3 cc, 10 units)

*(15) Razor blades

(16) Antidiarrhea pills

(17) Laxatives (Senna leaf tea or Casgara Sagrada are natural laxatives)

(18) Calamine lotion

*(19) Germicidal soap

(20) Bandana

(21) Scissors

(22) Tweezers

(23) Illustrations of CPR, tourniquet placement, pressure points, and splint arrangements

(24) Chapstick

(25) Needles, both heavy and light duty

(26) Rubber gloves

Signaling

(1) Radio, two-way voice or beacon

* (2) Mirror

(3) Whistle

(4) Flashlight (battery-less)

* (5) Flares

* (6) Smoke signals

(7) Illustrations of ground-to-air signals

Drinking Water

  (1) Canned water

  (2) Solar still

* (3) Plastic container/s

* (4) 6'x6' plastic material

* (5) Purification tablets (halazone)

  (6) Illustration of land solar still or sea solar still

  (7) Sponge

  (8) Plastic bags (2'x 4')

  (9) Illustration of vegetation still

Shelter Construction

  (1) Illustration of shelters for survival area

* (2) Knife (strong and sharp)

* (3) Whetstone/file

  (4) Axe

* (5) Wire saw

  (6) Chemical heat packs

  (7) Insulating blankets (wool)

  (8) Space blankets

* (9) Candles

*(10) Line

  (11) Mosquito netting

Food

* (1) Glucose sweets (hard candy)

* (2) Dried fruits

  (3) Boullion cubes

  (4) Flint and steel

  (5) Waterproof matches

  (6) Fishing gear

  (7) Gill net

* (8) Aluminum foil (one square yard, 2 each)

  (9) Slingshot

  (10) Wire (for snares)

Navigation

* (1) Map of area

* (2) Compass/ wrist compass

  (3) Illustrations of improvised footwear

  (4) Rope

  (5) Mountain-climbing gear

  (6) Machete

Selection of Survival Kit Items

The key to the types of items you will need in your survival kit is the environment. The key to how much you put in your kit and where you carry it is your mode of travel and your organic equipment. In preparing your survival kit, select items you can use for more than one purpose. If you have two items that will serve the same function, pick the one that you can also use for another function. Do not duplicate items as this will increase the size and weight of your kit. Your survival kit need not be elaborate. You need only functional items that will meet your needs and a case to hold the items. For the case you might use a band-aid box, a first aid case, an ammo pouch, or other suitable case, but it should be –

- Water repellent.
- Easy to carry.
- Durable, and
- Large enough to hold the items you need.

In your survival kit you should have-

- First aid items.
- Signaling items.
- Water and/or means to obtain potable water.
- Fire-starting items.
- Food and/or items to help you obtain food.
- Shelter items.

Questions:

1) From class

2) To class

In addition to the above listed reference material, the Honorable Min. Louis Farrakhan's Self-Improvement: The Basis for Community Development on 'Building the Will' is insightful and should be examined in addition to How to Eat to Live books 1&2 and Fall of America by The Most Honorable Elijah Muhammad. As with all endeavors, preparation is key in attaining success, and with regard to survival, preparation mentally, physically, and spiritually will be the determining factor between surviving and not surviving.

Bro. Mikaeel

Military Science

Survival Training (Part 2): First Aid, Preparation, Staying Healthy and Treating Injuries

Purpose: The purpose of this outline is to review injuries and introduce first aid procedures and treatments for injuries that could occur as a result of being injured during a survival situation. Review tips on staying healthy during a survival situation.

Learning Objectives: Upon completion of review of this outline the student will, with the aid of reference, identify first aid steps and methods in treating traumatic injuries, and staying healthy in survival situations.

References: How To Survive On Land And Sea – F. Craighead and J. Craighead, US Army Survival Manual – FM 21-76, US Air Force Search and Rescue Survival Training – AF Reg. 64-4

Body:

SECTION A

First Aid – Prevention, Other Health Concerns

When assembling your survival gear, you should give highest priority to your first aid kit, as you will very likely find yourself administering basic medical care, either to yourself or to others, in any struggle for survival. You should be aware of ways to prevent or, if necessary, to treat hypothermia (low body temperature), heatstroke, dehydration, and poisoning. The American Red Cross and other organizations offer both basic and advanced first aid courses. Such courses are highly recommended. This outline will briefly review basic first aid procedures and applications, emphasizing principles rather than specific treatments. A chart at the end will summarize particular health problems, their causes and symptoms, and the recommended treatment when professional help is not available.

Prevention

The adage, "An ounce of prevention is worth a pound of cure," is especially true in survival situations. It is imperative that you make every effort to prevent injuries and their complications such as blood loss, infection, and shock. In addition to completing first aid training courses and preparing a suitable first aid kit, you can immunize yourself against some diseases. Preventing health problems must be paramount in your mind.

Good personal hygiene, fitness, and common sense will help prevent many of the diseases associated with the stress of surviving, such as diarrhea, dysentery, and malaria. Do not become careless in

114

personal cleanliness or proper hygiene in the shelter area. Prevent poisoning by being careful in your selection and storage of food, and try not to let certain types of plant life come in contact with your skin.

Protective clothing will prevent cold-related problems such as frostbite, trench foot (a painful foot condition resembling frostbite), and hypothermia. Mosquito netting in tropical regions and sunglasses in the high glare of snow or desert may be necessary. Light-colored clothing will reflect the heat, protect from the ultraviolet sunrays, and retain moisture in very hot, dry areas. Not only will these preventive methods and others help head off many health problems but they will also significantly increase your comfort.

Other Health Concerns

Some threats to health may develop slowly. You should be aware of the dangers and act to prevent them. If you are not prepared for them, they may lead to unsuspected tragedy.

Strenuous Exertion – In any climate, severe headaches are common after strenuous, unaccustomed exertion. An aspirin will ease the pain, but the best relief is sleep or rest. If hungry, eat moderately of hot broth or sweets. Nibble at food more or less continually. If you're not hungry, don't force yourself to eat but wait until you are rested and your appetite returns. Try not to exert yourself over a long period of time without eating. Practicing the tenets of How to Eat to Live by The Most Honorable Elijah Muhammad, eating one meal a day or every two or three days along with fasting greatly aid the body in adapting to strenuous situations.

Care of the Feet – If you are going to be doing a lot of walking, you will have to take care that your feet do not develop blisters and sores that could impede your progress. Try to be sure that you are properly shod for any contingency when there's a chance that you may find yourself in harm's way. As you travel, bathe and massage your feet daily, if possible. Examine your feet for tell-tale redness or blisters. Do not puncture blisters, as this may cause infection. Apply an adhesive bandage for protection.

Care of the Digestive System – It is important that under the general stress of survival conditions, you strive to purify your water and cook your food. These two actions should help you considerably in your fight to ward off digestive problems. If you develop diarrhea, rest and fast but continue to take water. Overeating of fruit, especially green fruit, often leads to diarrhea and simply changing your diet will often make you feel better. If the opposite problem – constipation – afflicts you, do not be overly concerned. Provided you have plenty of water, your body functions will soon return to normal.

Preparation – Survival Medicines, Personal Hygiene

A particular individual may be quite capable of proceeding rationally on land but may tend to panic in a similar life-threatening situation on water. To short-circuit the panic button, accept and prepare to counter the unpredictability of intractable survival situations on land or sea. Avoid the "it can't happen to me" mentality. Rehearse emergency situations individually and with family or groups so that each person will know what his or her responsibility would be in such situations. Such a rehearsal could involve the actual use of some emergency equipment, for knowing that your equipment works can stave off panic at the last minute. If the unexpected happens, the sooner you can make the transition to acceptance of the situation, the better your chances of ultimate success. Accepting the new reality helps you to react constructively. Fear and panic subside as you turn your attention to the work that must be done. This work involves counteracting the effects of cold, fatigue, thirst, hunger, and pain. If any of these conditions gain the upper hand, it can weaken your will to prevail. You must fight to establish some measure of control, by means of your own will and your resourcefulness. However much you can accomplish with your body and powers of reason, you will be limited, perhaps dangerously so, without the right equipment. The final aspect of personal preparation is to educate yourself regarding your survival equipment.

Survival Medicines

<u>Procedures and Expedients</u> – Survival medicine encompasses procedures and expedients that are:

a. Required and available for the preservation of health and prevention, improvement, or treatment of injuries and illnesses encountered during survival.
b. Suitable for application by non-medical personnel to themselves or comrades in the circumstances of the survival situation.

Survival medicine is more than first aid in the conventional sense. It approaches final definitive treatment in that it is not dependent upon the availability of technical medical assistance within a reasonable period of time.

<u>Rules for Avoiding Illness</u> – In a survival situation, whether short-term or long-term, the dangers of disease are multiplied. Application of the following simple guidelines regarding personal hygiene will enable the survivor to safeguard personal health and the health of others:

a. All water obtained from natural sources should be purified before consumption.
b. The ground in a camp area should not be soiled with urine or feces. Latrines should be used, if available. When no latrines are available, individuals should dig "cat holes" away from the camp area and cover their waste.
c. Fingers and other contaminated objects should never be put into the mouth. Hands should be washed before handling any food or drinking water, before using the fingers in the care of the mouth and teeth, before and after caring for the sick and injured, and after handling any material likely to carry disease germs.

d. After each meal, all eating utensils should be cleaned and disinfected in boiling water.
e. The mouth and teeth should be cleansed thoroughly at least once each day. Most dental problems associated with long-term survival episodes can be prevented by using a toothbrush and toothpaste to remove accumulated food debris. If necessary, devices for cleaning the teeth should be improvised.
f. Bites and insects can be avoided by keeping the body clean, by wearing proper protective clothing, and by using a head net, improvised bed nets, and insect repellents.
g. Wet clothing should be exchanged for dry clothing as soon as possible to avoid unnecessary body-heat loss.
h. Personal items such as canteens, towels, toothbrushes, handkerchiefs, and shaving items should not be shared with others.
i. All food scraps, cans, and refuse should be removed from the camp area and buried.
j. If possible, a survivor should get 6-8 hours of sleep each night.

Personal Hygiene

In any situation, cleanliness is an important factor in preventing infection and disease; in a survival situation it becomes even more important. Of course, a daily shower with hot water and soap is ideal, but you can keep clean without this luxury. Use a cloth and soapy water to wash yourself. If water is scarce, take an "air" bath: Remove as much of your clothing as practical and expose your body to sun and air.

Keep Your Hands Clean. Germs on your hands can infect food and wounds. So be sure to wash your hands after handling any material that is likely to carry germs, after visiting the latrine, after caring for the sick, and before handling any food, food utensils, or drinking water. Keep your fingernails closely trimmed and clean, and keep your fingers out of your mouth.

Keep Your Hair Clean. Your hair can become a haven for fleas, lice, and other parasites or bacteria. Keeping your hair clean and trimmed will help you to avoid this danger. Fleas and lice live and feed on warm-blooded animals and are carriers of dangerous diseases. Louse powder is the best way to rid yourself of fleas and lice should you become infested. Other ways to rid yourself of these insects is to place your clothing in direct sunlight for a few hours or wash frequently in hot, soapy water.

Keep Your Clothing Clean. You should keep your clothing and bedding as clean as possible to reduce the chance of skin infection as well as to decrease the danger of parasite infestation. Clean your outer clothing whenever it becomes soiled. Wear clean underclothing and socks each day. If water is in short supply, "air" clean your clothing (shake, air, and sun for 2 hours). Turn your sleeping bag inside out after each use and fluff and air it.

Keep Your Teeth Clean. At least once each day, thoroughly clean your mouth and teeth with a toothbrush or dentifrice. If you don't have a toothbrush, make a "chewing stick." Find a twig about 8 inches long and ½ inch wide. Brush your teeth thoroughly with your chewing stick. Or wrap a clean strip of cloth around your finger and rub your teeth with it to wipe away food particles. To remove food stuck between your teeth, use a toothpick mad from a twig or use dental floss made from thread, string, or thin strips of bark or vine.

Take Care of Your Feet. To prevent serious foot trouble, break in your shoes prior to wearing them in any survival situation, wash and massage your feet daily, trim your toenails straight across, and check your feet for blisters. If you get a blister, do not open it. An intact blister is safe from infection. Apply a dressing around the blister, not on it. If the blister bursts, clean it and apply a bandage over it.

SECTION B

Staying Healthy – Caring for the Body (Physically/Psychologically)

Three of the most crucial factors in staying healthy are having adequate water and food, practicing good hygiene, and getting sufficient rest.

Your body loses water through normal body processes – sweating, urinating, and defecating. When the atmosphere is 68 degrees F, the average adult loses, and therefore requires, 2 to 3 liters (2 to 3 quarts) of water daily. In other circumstances, such as heat exposure, cold exposure, intense activity, high altitude, burns, or illness, your body may lose more water. This water must be replaced. Dehydration results from inadequate replacement of lost body fluids. It will decrease your efficiency in doing even the simplest task, and it will increase your susceptibility to severe shock if you are injured. Thirst is no indication of how much water you need, so even when you are not thirsty, drink small amounts of water regularly to prevent dehydration. If you are exerting a lot of energy or are under severe conditions, increase your water intake. Drink enough liquids to maintain a urine output of at least 1 pint every 24 hours. In a hot climate, you should drink 4 to 8 gallons of water a day. To treat dehydration, replace the body fluids that were lost. Drink any potable fluids available – water, fruit juices, tea and so forth.

CAUTION: *Do not use sea water or urine under any circumstances. Although they will satisfy thirst temporarily, they actually cause additional water loss from the body, promote dehydration, and if taken in sufficient quantity, will kill you.*

The adage "let your food be your medicine, and your medicine be your food" is crucial to understand and applicable especially in survival situations. There are numerous household items that can be used both as food and medicine. As well, there are numerous plants and herbs in the wild that can be used as food and medicine. Many modern medications come from refined herbs which become a "drug" when they are heated and processed. There is no cure in drugs, the Most Honorable Elijah Muhammad has taught us this and advised us decades ago that we should throw away the drugs in our medicine cabinets and let our food and fasting be our cure to our illnesses. Most prescription drugs have side effects and are taken to treat the symptoms of an illness, not the root cause. And, in most cases, cause more damage than the consumer may be aware of when taking such medications. As there are numerous publications of herbal books with natural remedies to illnesses, I will not list such but recommend that these books and information be added to your survival kit and that each person become familiar with such remedies.

Treating Injuries – Traumatic Injuries and Medical Emergencies

The accident that triggered the survival crisis may have caused some injuries of varying severity and type. Victims may be bleeding, their bones may be broken, or their bodies burned. Undoubtedly, all will suffer some degree of shock. Those persons administering first aid to victims must identify the injuries that exist, not only to others but to themselves as well. They must not become so involved in the treatment of others that they allow their own injuries to go unattended. Problems should be treated in the order of their seriousness, generally as follows:

(1) Lack of respiration or heart beat
(2) Severe external bleeding
(3) Wounds
(4) Fractures
(5) Burns
(6) Shock.

Heart or Respiratory Arrest

Regardless of the cause of heart or respiratory arrest – whether a sudden traumatic incident or the strain of a prolonged survival test – a person whose heart is not beating or who is not breathing must be revived quickly to prevent irreversible brain damage. When a person is unconscious and lying flat out on his back, the lower jaw may drop backward, possibly carrying the tongue with it and causing it to obstruct the air passage. Sometimes all that is necessary to clear the passage is for you to gently tilt his head backward as far as possible and to lift the neck or chin. This position of the head must be maintained at all times. When the victim is in this position, you should look, listen, and feel for whether he is breathing. If he does not seem to be breathing and does not respond to a tap on the shoulder or a shout, that person is a prime candidate for cardiopulmonary resuscitation (CPR), or mouth-to-mouth resuscitation and cardiac compression.

CPR. Cardiopulmonary resuscitation combines mouth-to-mouth breathing, which supplies oxygen to the lungs, with chest compressions, which squeeze the heart and artificially pump blood to the vital organs of the body. CPR courses are strongly recommended, as problems may develop with the naïve individual that can possibly lead to tragedy, while those fully trained in first aid will know exactly what to do.

To remember the correct step-by-step method of initiating CPR, the American Red Cross advises memorizing the phrase "A Quick Check."

A-Airway: Tip the head and check for breathing. Look, listen, and feel for signs of breathing for five seconds.

Quick: If the victim is not breathing, pinch his or her nose and place your mouth over the victim's mouth, or place your mouth over the victim's mouth and nose together; give four quick full breaths. Do not allow victim's lungs to completely deflate.

Babies and small children should receive gentle puffs.

Check: After administering the four quick breaths, check the pulse and respiration.

Check the pulse on the closest side of the neck by feeling the carotid artery.

Check the respiration by placing your ear close to the victim's mouth and listening. This check should last five seconds. The pulse of babies and small

Children may be checked on the inside of the upper arm by feeling the brachial artery.

(1) If the victim is not breathing but has a pulse, give mouth-to-mouth breath at a rate of twelve to fifteen breaths per minute (fifteen to twenty breaths per minute for children). Again, babies and small children should receive gentle puffs.

(2) If there are no signs of either pulse or respiration, then full CPR must be administered.
   (a) Ensure that the victim is horizontal and on a firm foundation.
   (b) Locate the lower one-third of the victim's sternum.
   (c) Place the heel of one hand on the sternum and the other hand over the first hand.
   (d) Compress an adult's sternum one and one-half to two inches at the rate of sixty to eighty compressions per minute. Proportionally smaller compressions are required for babies and small children (as little as one-half inch for babies) and the rate must be increased to eighty to one hundred compressions per minute.
   (e) Provide both mouth-to-mouth and chest compressions by establishing a cycle of fifteen compressions and two inflations. If two first aiders are available, a more effective cycle can be administered if one first aider compresses the chest and the other gives mouth-to-mouth on a five to one ratio. The person giving mouth-to-mouth should impose a breath on the fifth upstroke so that the rhythm of chest compressions is not interrupted. Cardiac massage and mouth-to-mouth may be given simultaneously on babies and small children by one first aider.

(3) If there is an obstruction in the airway, you will feel the resistance as you attempt to inflate the victim's lungs through mouth-to-mouth.

   (a) Recheck the position of the victim's head. Tipping the head back prevents the victim's tongue from blocking the airway.
   (b) If the airway is still blocked, roll the victim on his side toward the rescuer and hit the upper middle back four times. Return the victim to his back and administer four abdominal thrusts. Finally, clear the victim's mouth by probing with your finger.

Again, let us emphasize that this is only a description of CPR; there is no substitute for taking a course in first aid and CPR.

External Bleeding

Severe bleeding from any major blood vessel is extremely dangerous. Loss of two pints of blood, for example, can produce moderate shock, while loss of four pints can lead to severe shock and loss of six pints or more can result in death.

Types of Bleeding. The type of bleeding may be defined by its source: arterial, venous, or capillary. Arterial bleeding is the most serious and is recognized by its bright red color and distinct spurts or pulses which correspond to the heartbeat. A large volume of blood can be lost in a short time because of the high pressure in the arteries. Venous bleeding is blood that is returning to the heart and is recognized by its dark red or maroon color and steady flow. It is usually easier to control than arterial bleeding. Capillary bleeding results from cutting the very small vessels that actually supply blood to the tissues of the body and is recognized by its slow, oozing flow. All external bleeding must be cared for immediately in a survival situation.

Control of Bleeding. Direct pressure over the wound or broken blood vessel is the primary method of stopping external bleeding. No time should be lost in attempting to locate a sterile dressing if the bleeding is severe. The first aider should immediately press directly on the severed vessel using his or her bare finger or hand. While firmly pressing directly on the wound, attempt to locate a sterile dressing. If a sterile dressing is not available, use the cleanest cloth you have. Place the cloth firmly over the wound as you remove your hand.

Apply the dressing firmly with even pressure directly over the point of blood loss until the bleeding no longer shows through the dressing. Do not remove any dressing once it has been applied. If bleeding continues to permeate the dressing, apply a tighter bandage directly over the first one. The bandage is too tight, however, if the skin, fingernails, or toenails beyond the bandage start showing a bluish tinge, and the bandage should be loosened.

Bleeding may also be controlled by elevating the affected extremity as high above the heart as possible. Do not do this, however, if a fracture is involved. Pressure points may also be used to help control arterial bleeding. Pressure points are identified as those anatomical locations where the arteries are near the surface of the skin or directly over a bone. By locating the pressure point pertaining to the artery that supplies blood to the injured limb, you can apply pressure and control bleeding, especially arterial bleeding, in the entire limb. Do no use a pressure point for an arm or leg wound unless direct pressure and elevation will not stop the bleeding.

A common mistake is to think of a tourniquet as the primary means of arresting severe bleeding. In fact, a tourniquet is a last resort and should only be used if all other methods of controlling blood loss have failed. An improperly applied tourniquet may obstruct venous blood flow without totally stopping arterial flow, resulting in more profuse arterial bleeding than before the tourniquet was applied. Improperly applied tourniquets can also cause nerve damage.

A tourniquet is a wide constricting band placed around an extremity between the wound and the heart (two to four inches above the wound) and pulled just tight enough to stop the bleeding. A tourniquet that has been properly applied will stop the blood flow both to and from the wound. To correctly apply the tourniquet, follow this procedure:

(1) Place a dressing or pad, 3 to 4 inches wide, over the major artery leading to the wound.

(2) Wrap the tourniquet material (3 to 4 inches wide before tightening) around the extremity, directly over the pad.

(3) After two wraps, tie the ends together, then tie the material using a square knot around a stick.

(4) Slowly tighten the tourniquet by rotating the stick until the bleeding stops. Check to see that no blood is flowing from the wound.

(5) Secure the stick by tying one end of it to the limb with another bandage. The tightened tourniquet should be at least one inch in width.

(6) If you've applied the tourniquet to your own body, do not release once it has been applied. There is a possibility you may go into shock and be unable to re-secure it. If, however, you have applied the tourniquet to another, then it should be loosened every ten minutes for a period of one or two minutes to reduce the danger of losing a limb.

Wounds

   The care of open wounds is extremely important not only because of the potential for loss of blood but also because of the likelihood of infection. Infection results from contamination by and growth of bacteria, which may enter a wound at the time of injury or by contact with un-sterile materials such as clothing or bandages. Unwashed hands will undoubtedly introduce bacteria into the wound as you attempt to control the bleeding. Although speed is the primary consideration, you should try to wash your hands and, if possible, to sterilize your instruments and materials.

   Water to wash both the wound and your hands can be purified by boiling for three minutes at sea level and an additional minute for each one thousand feet thereafter. To sterilize instruments, hold them over an open flame and follow with an alcohol rinse.

   If severe bleeding is not a problem, gently wash the wounds prior to dressing. Remove the clothing around the wound and cleanse the whole area thoroughly. The wound itself, unless it is abdominal, should be irrigated – that is, pour sterile water over it – to remove any foreign matter. More infections are caused by foreign matter left in the wound than by the use of un-boiled water. If necessary, irrigate with un-boiled water. A pair of rubber gloves in your survival kit (be sure they are not packaged with talcum powder) makes a good syringe for washing wounds.

   Do not apply solutions such as Merthiolate, iodine, and Mercurochrome directly to open wounds. Rather carry an antiseptic solution such as benzalkonium chloride in your first aid kit and use that on open wounds. If sterile water for cleaning or benzalkonium chloride is not available, fresh urine may be used. After cleaning, the wound should be covered with a sterile dressing and bandage.

In the case of abdominal wounds, cleaning will probably introduce more infection than it prevents. Do not push organs back into the abdomen. Simply apply a dressing and keep it moist.

Open chest wounds often mean associated respiratory difficulties, which can be recognized by the victim's difficulty with breathing and perhaps hissing or sucking sounds coming from the wound. This type of wound should be made airtight immediately to restore normal respiratory function. Check both front and back before bandaging. Place plastic or rubber material directly over the open wound and cover with a sterile dressing. The dressing should not be removed once it has been applied.

Fractures

Fractures are classified as either open or closed. In an open fracture, the broken bone protrudes through the skin, while a closed fracture is a break in the bone without an associated break in the skin. Although recognizing a closed fracture is often difficult, pain, swelling, and disfiguration are some indications. If you are not sure whether a fracture exists, treat the bone as if it fractured.

The first aid for a fracture is to immobilize the affected area and the joints at either end. A splint carefully applied with bandages is the most common way to immobilize fractured bones. Any straight, firm piece of wood or metal can function as a splint; for a neck or foot fracture, use a rolled up blanket. Pad the splint with soft material such as cloth rags. Tie the splint to the body above and below the fracture.

Cracked ribs will give a sharp sensation of pain in the chest when moving, breathing, or straining. If a simple fracture, apply a snug bandage to restrict movement of the rib cage. If a compound fracture, immobilize the victim and treat for shock.

If medical help is not expected within a few hours, it is advisable for the first aider to set the bone before applying the splint. This should be done as soon after the accident as possible because swelling and muscle spasms will make it more difficult later. To set a broken bone, pull on the bone to straighten it. To set your own broken arm or leg, use the good arm or leg to apply traction, or, if additional traction is needed, make gravity work for you. Tie the limb to a fixed object and pull back. Alternatively, wedge a wrist or ankle into the fork of a tree or the niche of some rocks and then lean back with full weight of your body until you feel the bone snap into place. Then apply the padding and splint, which you have arranged for beforehand. If mobilization is not necessary, continued traction would help ensure correct alignment of the bone.

The first aid is similar for an open fracture except that the open wound must also be treated. Examine the ends of the broken bone for any dirt or debris, and, if dirty, rinse them with a saline solution of one-fourth teaspoon of salt per quart of sterilized water.

Burns

The aim of first aid treatment for serious burns is to control fluid loss and to prevent infection and shock. Minor burns (no broken skin) can be run under cold water. Check the first aid kit carefully for instructions and supplies for treating burns.

Burns can have a number of different causes. For chemical burns, quickly and thoroughly wash to remove all traces of the chemical. Remove any material such as clothing from in and around the burn.

Burns caused by steam or hot water (scalds) should be cooled immediately by immersion in cold water, as should burns caused by open flames or hot materials. Pieces of burned material such as clothing should not be removed from this type of burn because it would likely cause additional fluid loss.

All burns should be covered with a dry sterile dressing to prevent infection. Those with serious burns or burns over a large area of the body should be treated to prevent shock. Give aspirin (or herbal equivalent) to reduce the pain, keep the victim quiet and comfortable, lying down with feet elevated. Give plenty of fluids. Immobilize the burned limb by using splints or slings.

Shock

Injury-related shock is commonly called traumatic shock to differentiate it from other forms of shock, such as electric or insulin. Traumatic shock, which can result from any serious injury, is a reduction in the flow of oxygenated blood to the vital organs of the body. First aiders should make every effort to prevent shock when the situation indicates that it is likely. Severe stresses on the body, such as loss of blood, pain, poor circulation, or change in body temperature, cause shock and should be treated and, if possible, eliminated as soon as possible. Keep victims quiet, warm, comfortable, and lying down with their feet slightly elevated. If the victim's injuries permit, you may give water in small doses.

Questions:

1) From class

Summary: No booklet or reading material is a substitute for taking a certified First Aid/CPR course. It is highly recommended that such a course be undertaken along with any type of medical triage training available.

Bro. Mikaeel Muhammad

Section 5

The Conscientious Objector and The Captain

"...So let's put up the old weapons of this world and pick up the weapons of the next world – and that is truth... The little weapons that you think you have are just enough to get you killed. Our people only have these little weapons to kill one another. That's a shame. That's the wrong way the army should be trained."

– The Hon. Louis Farrakhan, *The Meaning of F.O.I.* (pgs 15-16)

Chapter 11

From Honorman to Conscientious Objector

What is a Conscientious Objector?

A *Conscientious Objector* is defined as a person who refuses to serve in the armed forces or bear arms on moral or religious grounds. In the Department of Defense (DoD) Directive 1300.6 (available in an online PDF format) dated May 5, 2007, conscientious objector is defined as:

3.1 Conscientious Objector: General. A firm, fixed, and sincere objection to participation in war in any form or the bearing of arms, by reason of religious training and/or belief. Unless otherwise specified, the term "Conscientious Objector" includes both Class 1-O and Class 1-A-O Conscientious Objectors.

3.1.1 Class 1-O Conscientious Objector. A member who, by reason of conscientious objection, sincerely objects to participation in military service of any kind in war in any form.

3.1.2 Class 1-A-O Conscientious Objector. A member who, by reason of conscientious objection, sincerely objects to participation as a combatant in war in any form, but whose convictions are such as to permit military service in a non-combat status.

The criteria laid out in this DoD directive/instruction is as follows:

5.1 General. The criteria set forth herein provide policy and guidance in considering applications for separation or for assignment to non-combatant training and service based on conscientious objection. Consistent with the national policy to recognize the claims of authentic Conscientious Objectors in the Military Service, an application for classification as a Conscientious Objector may be approved (subject to the limitations of paragraph 4.1) for any individual:

5.1.1 Who is conscientiously opposed to participation in war in any form;

5.1.2 Whose opposition is based on religious training and/or belief; and

5.1.3 Whose position is firm, fixed, sincere and deeply held.

5.2 Religious Training and/or Belief

5.2.1 In order to find that an applicant's moral and ethical beliefs are against participation in war in any form and are held with the strength of traditional religious convictions, the applicant must show that these moral and ethical convictions, once acquired, have directed the applicant's life in the way traditional religious convictions of equal strength, depth, and duration have directed the lives of those whose beliefs are clearly found in traditional religious convictions. In other words, the belief upon which conscientious objection is based must be the primary controlling force in the applicant's life.

5.2.2 A primary factor to be considered is the sincerity with which the belief is held. Great care must be exercised in seeking to determine whether asserted beliefs are honestly and genuinely held. Sincerity is determined by an impartial evaluation of the applicant's thinking and living in totality, past and present. Care must be exercised in determining the integrity of belief and the consistency of application. Information presented by the claimant can be sufficient to convince that the claimant's personal history reveals views and actions strong enough to demonstrate that expediency or avoidance of military service is not the basis of the applicant's claim.

Now, the above information was not available when I went through my conscientious objector process in the spring of 1992. As a matter of fact, even after having five favorable endorsements, a process that was supposed to take from 6-8 months was dragged out for a year and within that year I was threatened with reduction in rank and pay, court-martial, brig time, and even lied on, just to name a few trials. All the while, I continued selling *Final Call Newspapers* every Saturday on a corner in the military town outside of Camp Pendelton, California known as Oceanside.

From Unconscious to Conscious

Before hearing the Hon. Louis Farrakhan for the first time, live, December 8, 1990 at the Los Angeles Coliseum, I was looking for God. I had been looking for the reality of God since the age of 6 and as I was raised in the church (COGIC) I was steadily raising questions that weren't being answered satisfactorily. It was in 1988 that I had my first glimpse while catching the tail-end of a nightly news report in Washington, D.C. I was staying with my grandfather who lived in Palmer Park, Maryland and anticipating my time to ship off to Marine Corps Recruit Training Depot at Parris Island, South Carolina (September of that year). The news reporter was speaking about the "Fruit of Islam" of the Nation of Islam and how they had done what the police department failed to do when they cleaned up the drug-infested Paradise Apartments and Mayfair Manors in N.E. Washington, D.C. The thing that caught my attention however was the fact that the reporter stated that they accomplished driving out the dope-dealers "with NO weapons." When I heard that I thought, "God MUST be with those brothers!" And so it was this first image and impression of the Fruit of Islam that stuck in my head. However, prior to this I had enlisted in the Marine Corps at the age of 17 in October of 1987 during my senior year in High School in what is called the "Delayed-Entry Program." I had convinced my mother that if she didn't sign the waiver for me, as this was 3 months prior to my 18th birthday, that I would just sign up in January. The months I spent in the Delayed-Entry Program were to be counted against my reserve time required after enlistment, or something to that effect, and I was not scheduled to ship off to Boot Camp until September of 1988, giving me 11 months. During this 11 months I studied and prepared myself for Boot Camp, I was determined that I would graduate as Platoon Honorman. This distinguished honor awards the recipient with a meritorious promotion, choice in duty station, as well as earning the coveted Marine Corps "Dress Blues" uniform.

I accomplished exactly what I set out to do and graduated December 1, 1988 from MCRD Parris Island, South Carolina as Honorman of Platoon 1094. Next, I set my eyes on graduating first out of my MOS school, which for me was the School of Communications at Camp Lejeune, North Carolina. After graduating first in my class from the School of Communications and receiving a meritorious promotion to the rank of Lance Corporal (E-3), earning me a choice in duty station, along with a few trials, I chose to serve on the West Coast because I had never been to California or anywhere else besides my travels up and down the East Coast from Florida to Rhode Island. But another incident would impression me that occurred in 1989. It was after a press conference given by the Hon. Louis Farrakhan (which I did not see then) in Washington, D.C. that a strange object was visible at night over top of the Capitol for a few nights. It appeared as a red-colored disk and was first reported on the nightly news but then given no more coverage after the first night, even though it was seen for more than one night. I later came to learn that this was a "baby-plane" that the Most Hon. Elijah Muhammad and the Hon. Louis Farrakhan spoke about. I would see more of these in the future.

A few months after arriving at Camp Pendelton, California in March of 1990, I ended up assigned to the School of Communications, which was located at Camp Margarita at the time, to be a communications instructor. Graduating two classes I was immediately called back to my main unit (1st Battalion, 9th Marines) for deployment to the Gulf as the "Operation: Desert Shield" had now become "Operation: Desert Storm." I had been listening to conscious-rap group Public Enemy which influenced me greatly and led me to read speeches by Malcolm X as well as his autobiography. I was studying books put out that spoke on the Counter-Intelligence Program (COINTELPRO) and their involvement in the assassinations of both Malcolm X and Dr. Martin Luther King. I had also visited Muhammad Mosque #8 by September of this same year (1990). I had purchased 'Fall of America' by the Most Hon. Elijah Muhammad, and then later 'Our Savior Has Arrived,' and finally found a copy of 'Message to the Blackman in America,' which was available at Pyramid Bookstore on Euclid Ave. at the time in San Diego. I was stocking up on books such as 'The Souls of Black Folk' by W.E.B. DuBois, and 'How Europe Underdeveloped Africa' by Walter Rodney, and the list goes on. I was becoming "CONSCIOUS." In October I was promoted to Corporal (E-4) the day before I returned to my unit. Now an NCO, or non-commissioned officer, achieving said rank in 2 years of my enlistment time I felt as though I was on my way in accomplishing my military career goals. My next sights were deciding on applying for Drill Instructor School to become a Drill Instructor (trainer and maker of Marines) or Force Reconnaissance. After either one I intended to apply for the Marine Enlisted College Entry Program (MECEP) and go to college and receive a commission as an officer and finish out my career as a respected "Mustang" (the name given to Marines who serve as both enlisted and officer). But as I was becoming conscious, all those career goals changed the moment I heard the Hon. Louis Farrakhan speaking live in Los Angeles at the L.A. Coliseum December, 8th. His topic was 'Save the Black Family' and he spoke on the Gulf War and in the manner in which he spoke I looked at him as a General.

I left that speech with a weight on my head, walking in the valley of decision. The more I was learning, the less "gung-ho" I was feeling about the Marine Corps. In February of 1991, while conducting training exercises in preparation for my deployment overseas, my unit went to Fort Ord which was an Army base just outside of San Francisco. There was a mock town built on the base, it had 3-5 story buildings, homes, streets, and a sewer pipe network underneath the town. There were 'Urban Warfare' classes and training conducted and door-to-door breaches and drills done as well. The odd thing about this scenario is that in my head this town looked NOTHING like any town that we would encounter in the deserts of Arabia. This town looked EXACTLY like "Anytown USA." By this time I had changed my religion to Islam, even had it designated on my "dog-tags."

I had found copies of 'How To Eat To Live' (books 1&2) by the Messenger on a visit to the Los Angeles area to hear a debate by Bro. Min. A. Khallid Muhammad and later a lecture he gave at Muhammad's Mosque #27. After reading both books, and knowing my unit was about to conduct another training exercise in the desert of El Centro, California for 30 days, I decided to use that time to apply the teachings of the dietary law espoused by the Messenger and began eating one meal a day during the course of this exercise. I had also purchased a Holy Qur'an and read each of the 30 parts during the 30 days of the training exercise. During this training exercise I was also privy to serving in the Command Post (CP) tent and on one particular night-fire exercise observed a remote-controlled HUMM-V with a remote-controlled machine gun turret being operated.

As my deployment time came closer, I thought to miss the entire movement, which would have subjected me to a court-martial. But it had been reported that some Muslim brothers allegedly tried to take over a Navy ship in a mutinous effort and the Messenger's books were found on them or amongst their possessions. This, however, was not truly the case but the atmosphere against Muslims in the military was building. In constant prayer, I deployed with my unit aboard the LHA-class (Landing Helo Assault) ship U.S.S. Peliliu, which was like a miniature carrier, manned by 4,000 personnel (2,500 sailors and 1,500 Marines). Because of the atmosphere building up against Muslims (especially outspoken ones like myself), I was separated from my unit and assigned to "Ship's-platoon" in charge of loading and offloading the cargo hold of the ship. This was actually a blessing for me because there were so many NCO's that we arranged a duty schedule of 1-day on and 2-days off for the NCOs. This meant I had even more time to study and train, and I did a lot of studying and training. There was a Petty Officer Anthony Willis (who later became Anthony 19X in Chicago I believe) who I met from a study group several of us Muslims formed aboard the ship. Bro. Anthony had the "Self-Improvement" Study Guides 1-17 of the Hon. Louis Farrakhan and I had Study Guide 18 which I had picked up in Long Beach before deployment. So this brother and I were study partners the entire 6 month duration of our deployment.

When we went to Hong Kong, I traveled across the river to Kowloon and found the Masjiid. Following other Muslims in and trying my hardest to mimic everything they did without looking out of place (I know I had to have looked awkward), I performed ablution and followed a brother into the sanctuary and joined the congregation for salat for the first time. Seeing that I was new and unlearned, a brother gave me a small book/pamphlet on how to perform salat. It was translated into French and was written for children but I could follow along with the pictures and the phonetically spelled out Arabic.

A Profound Understanding of Islam

By the time we arrived in Saudi Arabia, and after perusing the little French pamphlet on salat over and over again, I was eager to make salat in the masjiids in Arabia. I met Muslims in Dubai who embraced both Bro. Anthony and myself and they treated us like we were long lost relatives. At one point we were taken to one of the largest masjiids at that time in Dubai of whose Imam was the cousin of a brother who was giving us a tour of the city. We had a long discussion through an interpreter (as the Imam spoke no English) and we were asked numerous questions about being Muslims in America, to which I had to respond that I was new to Islam. When asked my name, the Imam expressed that I was named after the archangel and that in their teachings this angel "Mika'el" had 70,000 wings. I asked, "What was the significance of the 70,000?" Why not 700, or 7,000? And what was the significance of the "wings?" They tried to explain that it was all metaphor but they didn't know the answers and that since the angels were beyond our realm I could not comprehend. I immediately recalled what I heard Dr. Khallid say from his lecture "The White Man is Still The Devil," of which I had the tape, about the hadith in which the Prophet Muhammad (SAAWS) and his companions were around a fire and a man coming to them joining them and questioning them on points of the faith of Islam. The Prophet asked the question after the mysterious figure's departure, "Do you know who that man was? That MAN was the angel Jabril." He called the angel a man. So when I stated such, and after interpretation, the Imam spoke for a minute or two and when it was interpreted it was stated that "To be such a baby in Islam you have such a profound understanding." I thought to myself, "What little I know I received from reading the teachings of the Most Hon. Elijah Muhammad, and what I understand came from how the Hon. Louis Farrakhan represents it, so this MUST be the true Islam and right for me." Here was this Imam, able to recite the Holy Qur'an back and forth from memory, studied since the age of 4, telling me I had a profound understanding. I was starting to emerge from the valley of decision at this point.

Upon return to the states I immediately began going back to the mosque in San Diego, ironically the same mosque Malcolm X had helped establish, and shortly thereafter had met bro. Capt. Salim Muhammad. A few months later, I decided that I could not continue with my career pursuits in the Marine Corps and that my destiny lay in being a part of God's army and helping the Hon. Louis Farrakhan. I took a month of leave and went home to D.C. to visit with family and to consult my god-father who was a retired Marine Master Gunnery Sergeant with 23 and a half years of service. I knew he was an admirer of Minister Farrakhan but I initially thought he wouldn't understand the decision I was resolved to make. I also knew that my god-father was a Shriner and figured he knew somebody that could help me, and he did. One of his fellow Shriners and Marine partner from his Vietnam service happened to be in a pivotal position which could aid me and so he called him and allowed me to speak to him directly. I was made to understand the process of 'Conscientious Objector' and instructed on how to handle the scrutiny and threats that would come against me.

I returned from leave and one morning woke up resolved to declare myself a 'Conscientious Objector' seeking separation from the Marines. This was one of THE biggest challenges I had ever faced. To be trained to kill, drilled relentlessly, serve in a combat unit, be an NCO (a highly respected leadership position and considered the backbone of the Marine Corps), and declare that you refuse to kill or participate in war is to throw yourself in the midst of wolves and declare you are no longer part of the pack. It is perceived to be the act of a coward, which I was most certainly not, and just like wolves will turn on their own and kill them, I had to prepare for the same type of retribution which could be sought against me for seemingly turning my back on the Marine Corps. But Allah blessed me to be resolute in my convictions and I was steadfast in prayer and study and having to interview up the chain of command from the company level to the base commander I was given all five favorable endorsements saying that I should be discharged based on my sincerity and religious convictions and principles and so I was finally discharged with a 'General Under Honorable Discharge' status. This is only one grade below an 'Honorable Discharge' and I could not receive that because by this time I had served 4 and half years of my 6-year enlistment contract.

Initially, I thought to write about how to go about becoming a Conscientious Objector, especially after the Hon. Louis Farrakhan has spoken on it numerous times as of late. However, as I am writing this it came to me how this personal trial helped strengthen my convictions and faith in Islam and I would not be the person I have grown to be (and continuing to grow into becoming) had I not gone through all of this. So to publish such would serve no purpose, as each individual who may be serving in the armed forces will not be able to successfully achieve separation in the exact same manner. And those who are not in the armed forces who may be, at some time in the future, called to serve will not have the same experience either and may be subjected to more than what the legendary boxing champion Muhammad Ali faced when he declared himself a conscientious objector during the Vietnam War era. So I wrote and shared a little of my experience to show that it is possible, as I am an example, and that as my mentor and captain in the Nation of Islam, Capt. Salim Muhammad (May Allah be pleased with his service) would say, "Take what you have learned and use it to do what you need to do in the name of Allah, and you'll be successful."

War Is A Racket

In Marine Corps Boot Camp training there is history, as well as traditions, customs and courtesies that are required information a recruit is drilled on and made to commit to memory. There is not a Marine living today who does not know something about the 'Battle at Bellieu Woods' or the 'Battle at Tarawa', or such names as "Chesty" Puller. Of all of this information, one of the most prominent names made to be committed to memory is that of the twice-awarded 'Medal of Honor' recipient, Major General (2-stars) Smedley D. Butler, THE most decorated officer in the history of the Marine Corps. However, what is little known, or even talked about, is the exploits of this highly decorated Marine Corps General AFTER his 33 years of military service.

Maj. Gen. Smedley Butler is the author of a book published in 1935 entitled, '*War Is A Racket*'. In the opening of chapter 1 of his book he states:

"W A R is a racket. It always has been. It is possibly the oldest, easily the most profitable, surely the most vicious. It is the only one international in scope. It is the only one in which the profits are reckoned in dollars and the losses in lives.

A racket is best described, I believe, as something that is not what it seems to the majority of people. Only a small "inside" group know what it is about. It is conducted for the benefit of the very few, at the expense of the very many. Out of war a few people make huge fortunes.

In the World War a mere handful garnered the profits of the conflict. At least 21,000 new millionaires and billionaires were made in the United States during the World War. That many admitted their huge blood gains in their income tax returns. How many other war millionaire falsified their income tax returns no one knows."

Though this was written in 1935 it could easily be applicable to today, the game has not changed, merely the players. Maj. Gen. Butler was known for blowing the whistle on what he exposed as a fascist plot to seize the U.S. Government by Wall Street. The details of this are outlined in several sources such as George Seldes' book in 1947 '*1000 Americans*', the out-of-print tome of Jules Archer entitled '*The Plot to Seize the White*

House' (1973) as well as the *McCormick/Dickstein Commission* report (which was suppressed in its original release). From the Editorial Note of George Seldes' book, as expressed in the introduction given by Adam Parfrey to '*War Is A Racket*', Seldes' Editorial Note states:

General Smedley Butler testified before a Congressional Committee that several Wall Street bankers, one of them connected with J.P. Morgan and Co., several founders of the American Legion (one of the DuPonts was on the board of directors -MDSM) plotted to seize the government of the United States shortly after President Roosevelt established the New Deal. The press, with a few exceptions, suppressed the news. Worse yet, the McCormick-Dickstein Committee suppressed the facts involving the big business interests, although it confirmed the plot which newspapers and magazines had either refused to mention or had tried to kill by ridicule.

Time Magazine published an article in December of 1934 in an attempt to ridicule Maj. Gen. Butler as he was blowing the whistle on Wall Street (et al), and interestingly enough, *Time* Magazine was controlled by J.P. Morgan & Company at that time.

Also, before there was an "Occupy Wall Street" movement, in May of 1932 Washington, D. C. was occupied by out-of-work World War I veterans who were demanding the promised $1,000 "war bonus" desiring that it be paid sooner than the 1945 date given to them. As a major dust storm had ravaged the mid-west, a result of soil erosion due to farmers not properly rotating crops and such, and the so-called Great Depression had hit, these veterans needed their bonus now more than ever. And so tens of thousands of these veterans occupied, set up tents and camped out at what would come to be known as "Hoover-ville" which was the Anacostia area of D.C. General MacArthur, along with General George Patton, used newer U.S. Army soldiers as a contingent against the veterans in an effort to gain control of D.C. as these veterans expressed their anger in what would be called a "death march." They initially called Maj. Gen. Smedley Butler in to handle the veterans, as he always had a good rapport with troops and was highly respected. But, when Maj. Gen. Butler arrived, he sided with the veterans and sat with them all night, ate with them, and counseled them on how they should better organize themselves to be more effective, gain their demands, and avoid potential bloodshed. Obviously, this annoyed the "higher-ups" and so Gen. MacArthur and company were called in to deal with the disgruntled veterans. As a result of MacArthur's efforts, hundreds of veterans were injured and two died, including an infant, and Hoover-ville was burned to the ground.

There is more to Maj. Gen. Smedley Butler's escapades post-Marine Corps, but I bring this all to light to show that here is one of the most highly-decorated officers of the most highly respected branch of service under the Department of Defense of the United States government who, after 33 years of service, demonstrated the actions of what could be considered a "conscientious" person who objected to war and the mistreatment of people even after serving in the so-called Devil's military. He was not brain-washed by his military service. He stood up on principle and defended what was right and exposed what was wrong, he also wrote an "Amendment for Peace" to the Constitution which proposed anti-war legislation as well as the following:

1. *"The removal of members of the land armed forces from within the continental limits of the United States and the Panama Canal Zone for any cause whatsoever is prohibited.*
2. *The vessels of the United States Navy, or of the other branches of the armed service, are hereby prohibited from steaming, for any reason whatsoever except on an errand of mercy, more than five hundred miles from our coast.*
3. *Aircraft of the Army (the Air Force was formed from the Army Air Corps), Navy and Marine Corps is hereby prohibited from flying, for any reason whatsoever, more than seven hundred and fifty miles beyond the coast of the United States. Such an amendment would be absolute guarantee to the women of America that their loved ones never would be sent overseas to be needlessly shot down in European or Asiatic or African wars that are no concern of our people*

Such an amendment, linked with adequate naval and military defenses at home, would guarantee everlasting peace to our nation."

When I first heard the Hon. Louis Farrakhan speak live in December of 1990 he was laying out the agenda of the Bush Administration in the Gulf War. No news media ever disputed with his words, they just continued to attempt to smear his image with "anti-semitism" rhetoric. But never did they, or have they, disputed, contended with, or called him an outright liar for his words. Because he was/is a hundred percent right and exact. In chapter 5 (entitled 'To Hell With War!') of his book, 'War Is A Racket', mind you again that this book was published in 1935, Major Gen. Smedley Butler states:

"Looking back, Woodrow Wilson was re-elected president in 1916 on a platform that he would "keep us out of war." Yet, five months later he asked Congress to declare war on Germany.

In that five-month interval the people had not been asked whether they had changed their minds. The 4,000,000 young men who put on uniforms and marched or sailed away were not asked whether they wanted to go forth to suffer and die.

Then what caused our government to change its mind so suddenly? Money.

... Had secrecy been outlawed as far as war negotiations were concerned, and had the press been invited to be present at that conference [allied commission called by the then President Wilson – MDSM], or had the radio been available to broadcast the proceedings, America never would have entered the World War. But this conference, like all war discussions, was shrouded in the utmost secrecy.

When our boys were sent off to war they were told it was a "war to make the world safe for democracy" and a "war to end all wars." [sound familiar?!? – MDSM]

Well, eighteen years after, the world has less of a democracy than it had then.

He further summated that:

"The chief aim of any power at any of these conferences has been not to achieve disarmament in order to prevent war but rather to endeavor to get more armament for itself and less for any potential foe.

There is only one way to disarm with any semblance of practicability. That is for all nations to get together and scrap every ship, every gun, every rifle, every tank, every war plane. Even this, if it were at all possible, would not be enough.

The next war, according to experts, will be fought not with battleships, not by artillery, not with rifles and not with guns. It will be fought with deadly chemicals and gases.

Secretly each nation is studying and perfecting newer and ghastlier means of annihilating its foes wholesale. Yes, ships will continue to get built, for the shipbuilders must make their profits. And guns still will be manufactured and powder and rifles will be made, for the munitions makers must make their profits. And the soldiers, of course, must wear uniforms, for the manufacturers must make their war profits too.

But victory or defeat will be determined by the skill and ingenuity of our scientists.

If we put them to work making poison gas and more and more fiendish mechanical and explosive instruments of destruction, they will have no time for the constructive job of building a greater prosperity for all peoples. By putting them to this useful job, we can all make more money out of peace than we can out of war – even the munitions makers.

So ... I say, "TO HELL WITH WAR!"

This, coming from the most highly decorated Marine Corps officer in history. So for all of you who thought you understood the mindset and training of those of us who served in the armed forces, you really don't have and have not had, a hint of an iota of a clue. Unfortunately, Maj. Gen. Smedley Butler, nick-named "Old Gimlet Eye" and "The Fighting Quaker", checked himself into a veterans hospital in June of 1940 after becoming sick a few weeks earlier. His doctor described his illness as an incurable condition of the upper gastro-intestinal (GI) tract. And, Maj. Gen. Smedley Butler died June 21, 1940 in the Naval Hospital in Philadelphia, Pennsylvania just about a month before his 59th birthday (July 30, 1881). This was a year and half before the December 7th bombing of Pearl Harbor in Hawaii in 1941. A man like Maj. Gen. Smedley Butler could have perceived the machinations of those whose hands were behind this incident that triggered World War II and called them out. How many millionaires and billionaires came into existence behind this war? How many millionaires and billionaires came into existence behind the Korean War? Vietnam? Granada? The Gulf? Afghanistan? It is my belief that a man like Maj. Gen. Smedley Butler would have pointed these things out.

It is also my belief that a Marine Corps veteran like Maj. Gen. Smedley Butler would have been supportive of individuals like myself who became Conscientious Objectors and stood on point No. 10 of the Muslim Program of the Most Hon. Elijah Muhammad wherein it states:

10. *We BELIEVE that we who declare ourselves to be righteous Muslims, should not participate in wars which take the lives of humans. We do not believe this nation should force us to take part in such wars, for we have nothing to gain from it unless America agrees to give us the necessary territory wherein we may have something to fight for.*

And it is my belief that the Hon. Louis Farrakhan knows, and has known, exactly what he is talking about when he suggests to the youth to become Conscientious Objectors, but make sure they live a life reflective OF a Conscientious Objector.

Chapter 12

The "Ahk," Salim: A Dedication To A Mighty Captain

Brother Captain Salim Muhammad

Sunrise – August 7, 1944

Sunset – December 4, 2009

By far, the most influential Muslim in my life that I have had direct contact and dealings with would be my Captain in the Nation of Islam, Bro. Capt. Salim Muhammad (may Allah be pleased with his service). Affectionately known as "the Ahk," which means "brother" in the Arabic language (sister is "uhkt" but that doesn't sound pleasing to make that sound when speaking to a woman, smile). I am well aware that there are multitudes of people who could tell stories of their inter-relations with that brother but since I haven't seen anyone else write on such I decided to dedicate a chapter to him based on how I was affected by him.

I was a processing brother in San Diego, California, the year was 1991 early December. I was still enlisted in the U.S. Marines and had just returned from a tour overseas with the 15th Marine Expeditionary Unit (MEU) on what is known as a "West-Pac" float (western-pacific). This tour had taken me across the Pacific Ocean to Subic Bay, Phillipines right after Mt. Pinatubo had erupted (4-5 ft of ash everywhere and no power), Hong Kong, Singapore, and Saudi Arabia. This was just about a year after I had heard the Hon. Louis Farrakhan speak live at the L.A. Coliseum in December of 1990. I had been studying with another brother on ship (USS Peleliu) and I was eager to get back to attending the mosque and continuing the process I had begun. Bro. Captain Salim had just brought peace to a hold-over meeting that had erupted after a long period of time and went late into the night, and it was my understanding that he wasn't intending to stay in San Diego long as he was just visiting Sis. Gwendolyn, his wife at the time. I was told he was urged by the Hon. Louis Farrakhan to remain at Muhammad Mosque #8 for a period of time and see if he could help make some needed changes. From studying past VHS tapes of lectures by the Hon. Louis Farrakhan and always seeing Capt. Salim in the background doing security, especially when there was no "E-Team" it was clear to me who this man was. A few months later, in 1992, I started my Conscientious Objector process seeking separation from the Marine Corps (as discussed in chapter 10). After receiving five endorsements, all in favor of my separation as a conscientious objector, and awaiting my separation orders and discharge it was Capt. Salim who encouraged me to write my Savior's Letter. And so I did, it was received, and all I needed was proof of my separation from the military and I was ready to recite my Student Enrollment and Actual Facts.

True Brotherhood Demonstrated

During the hard trials of being in Conscientious Objector status, and going through a rough period in my second marriage it was Capt. Salim who would always remind me that the Holy Qur'an states "Hard trials are necessary to establish truth." Capt. Salim had a way of teaching and training that gave you the encouragement to persevere and know that you would come out on top if you were indeed sincere, faithful, and doing whatever you were doing of righteous conduct in the Name of Allah. But the incident which created a life-long bond between he and I occurred after I became a registered-Believer in 1993, after which Capt. Salim deputized me as one of his lieutenants and put me to work. At this particular time I was the so-called "paper-captain" under Capt. Salim and I had a key to the mosque and was there to open the mosque and set up the sanctuary for every meeting 4 days a week and sometimes on Saturday mornings for the M.G.T. class. I was struggling financially, as well as everyone else, was drawing unemployment from the military which amounted to about $633 per month, and stretching dollars until they snapped. Selling FCNs and bean pies helped a lot to supplement some income coming in as I struggled through finding steady work.

It was a Wednesday night and when I left my home the low-fuel indicator light was on in my '88 Ford Bronco II, and it had been on for some time so I knew I was on fumes but I knew I had enough to make it to the mosque to open the doors. I had just sent off the monies for the next edition of the Final Call Newspaper the night before and there was $20 left over of which I had not calculated the nickel off the paper which the captains receive. When I arrived at the mosque, thanking Allah I didn't get stranded, but not knowing how I was going to make it home, I figured in my head I would walk whatever remaining distance to my home my truck left me. Capt. Salim came in 10 minutes after I opened up the doors and after he went to his office I handed him the $20 which was in the denomination of two ten dollar bills and explained to him that it was left over after I sent the correct monies in to Chicago for the next edition of FCN. I turned and walked away to begin sweeping the floor of the sanctuary and Capt. Salim interrupted me and the conversation went as so:

"Ahk, here, take this brother," he handed me a $10 bill. I said, "no sir, that's your money sir from the FCNs." He said, "brother, take this, you need it." I responded in the negative again. He grabbed my wrist, thrust the bill in my hand and said sternly, with his one nostril flaring and edge of his top lip curling, "I said, take this you need it brother." I hung my head, with a puzzled look on my face, and a tear started forming in my left eye. I said, "brother Captain, what would make you say that?" Captain Salim replied, "Do you think I could befriend a man like the Leader (Hon. Louis Farrakhan), travel and secure him all these years and some of his spirit and character NOT rub off on me? The Leader is very sensitive to other's needs, and brother I have become sensitive in that way too, you don't show a lot of emotion but I know the look on your face and I see pain. It ain't a lot of pain but there is something there, and the Messenger taught us that when my brother's pinky toe hurt's then MY pinky toe is supposed to hurt. That's what happens when you spend a lot of time with your brother, you become in tune with him. Ya'see? The Messenger said when your brother has a bowl of bean soup you automatically have half, so the moment you gave me the $20 half of it belonged to you."

At this point that tear found its way down my cheek and I was shaking my head in disbelief. I said, "brother Captain, you just don't know, I came here on fumes not even knowing how I was going to get back home tonight, so I did need this." He said, "I know ahk, I could tell that look because you look how I feel at times, I'm low on ends right now too. Hell, we're both broke, busted, disgusted....but we can be trusted," he grinned, and that changed my demeanor. He said, "Don't worry brother, Allah is going to bless us both, the Book says 'Hard trials are necessary to establish truth' and we just got to get through these hard trials, ya'unnastand." From that point on, anyone and everyone would, and had, a hard time saying anything negative to me about Captain Salim. He was truly an example to me about what brotherhood in the Nation of Islam, and the world, is supposed to be.

When Capt. Salim was preparing to leave San Diego, to begin traveling with the Hon. Louis Farrakhan again, he came to me and said he needed to improve his conditioning so that he would be fit to secure our Leader and wanted to work out at the gym where I had a membership at the time. So for nearly three months I arose for prayer and picked up Capt. Salim in time for us to walk into the Bally's Fitness facility by 6am for four days a week. Not long after, it was a brother Stevie Muhammad (MM#8) and myself who helped Capt. Salim move his family (at the time, Sis. Gwendolyn Muhammad) from San Diego to Oklahoma. It was one of the best road trips ever, but upon return the realization that my captain was leaving for good was settling in. I sat on the front steps of his home the day he loaded the last of his items from his house into his car, I was upset. He sat down on the stairs with me and told me, "Don't worry ahk! I'm not abandoning you to all this madness, I'm going to send help your way. Stay strong soldier, Allah is with you, you'll see." This "help" did arrive months later and he called me at the mosque in San Diego to speak with me and remind me that he had not forgotten about me.

Capt. Salim Makes A Way, Again

Fast-forward to 2004, I had left San Diego six years prior and moved back to my hometown and after four years there with my second marriage going a similar direction as my first I ended up moving to Las Vegas, Nevada in an effort to compromise with my ex-wife. I was beyond frustrated after several incidences which had occurred in San Diego (the "madness" Capt. Salim was referring to), as well as with the study group I had attended in Princes Georges County, Maryland just outside of D.C. I was embittered to the point that it was two years before I even thought about going to the mosque while residing in Las Vegas. I continued to listen to the Hon. Louis Farrakhan throughout but I was determined that things had really changed since the Million Man March, and not for the better. I had recalled traveling to the mosque in Las Vegas back in 1994 on a return road-trip from hearing the Hon. Louis Farrakhan speak at the Jacob Javits Center in New York (the same historical speech where he announced he was calling a million men to march on Washington, D.C.). So for some particular reason I jumped off the I-15 and headed up D Street towards Jackson and found my way to the mosque. There was a crack in the front glass door which extended from one corner at the top to the opposite corner at the bottom. In addition to the debris that was all around the backside of the building, I remember thinking, "Damn, if it looks like this on the outside this is a reflection of the believers on the inside, cracked up with debris around, and I don't want any part of whatever they are doing." I drove off and didn't look back.

I was still in contact with a few Believers and Bro. Tyrone Sheriff, along with Bro. Sean Muhammad (whom I both originally soldiered with in San Diego) had just come up to Las Vegas and after a long martial arts training session we dialogued and agreed that we would rededicate ourselves to striving to do something using our talents to affect needed changes in the Nation of Islam to the best of our abilities. It was shortly after this training session that I received a phone call from Bro. Sean who informed me that he had just spoken to Capt. Salim and that the captain wanted me to call him at the Palace in Phoenix. I had not seen Capt. Salim since the Hon. Louis Farrakhan spoke in Washington, D. C. at Howard University just a couple years before. And so, I called my captain, and we spoke for a bit and I shared with him my frustrations and some of the incidences that happened and what I observed when I considered going to the mosque in Las Vegas. He in turn told me that he wanted me to come to the mosque in Phoenix the following Sunday, along with Bro. Sean and Bro. Tyrone, not to worry about a "traveling letter," and that we would talk more face to face.

So after the mosque meeting the following Sunday in Phoenix we broke bread at a restaurant Capt. Salim knew I could eat at, as I was pretty much the only vegetarian out of the crew at the time. We all talked about the current affairs that had affected us and at some point in the conversation Capt. Salim turned to me and said, "And you brother, I listened to you speaking about the crack in the door of the mosque and such, but what you have to understand is the military trained you to have an eye for detail, everybody doesn't have that. And so instead of sitting on the outside of the mosque observing these things you need to be on the inside pointing these things out and helping to do something to fix the problems. You are right, the building is a reflection of the people but how are they going to change if you are not helping things to change?" Then he looked at all of us and stated, "You know what you all did? You let go of the plow. You know farmer in the old days using the plow had a hard job, it's hard work guiding a plow behind a jackass. If you let the plow go the jackass is either going to make crooked lines all over or not move at all. So driving the jackass from behind, you have to put your shoulder and back into it to keep the plow straight and you get calloused hands." Then he tapped me on the leg and said, "And you ahk, you were my lieutenant, how many times had I shared with you the trials I have had securing the Leader? I told you they even blocked the Leader from seeing the Messenger when he was called to Chicago from New York BY the Messenger." He continued, "This is what I want you all to do, come to my house, I have something to show you all, you need to see this, and then you can get on the road before it gets too late."

We went to Capt. Salim's home and he put on the BET special which featured the Hon. Louis Farrakhan and his family talking about the trials the Minister faced when he was on his death bed and fighting the effects from the radiation treatment he received. I had seen this special before but for some reason, watching it with Capt. Salim made it have a different affect on me as Capt. Salim opened up even more about some of the "hard trials" the Hon. Louis Farrakhan has gone through. By the time the credits rolled there was not a dry eye in the room. I was thinking how selfish it was for me to think that I had been going through any trial worth complaining about and here was this man, the Hon. Louis Farrakhan, at deaths door, and constantly watched by counter-intelligence agents as well as dealing with all of the problems of the Nation of Islam as well as people outside of the organization. It was after this meeting that, after words of encouragement by Capt. Salim, I decided I was going back into the mosque and refused to be denied the opportunity to use my talents and skills to help build the brotherhood and strive to fulfill the pledges I signed my name to ('Pledge card') when first accepting the teachings of the Most Hon. Elijah Muhammad. I gave my word to Capt. Salim that I was NOT going to let go of the plow again. And so here I am, at the writing of my third volume of 'On Military Science,' reflecting on my time spent with Capt. Salim.

Last Words Before And After His Transition

I last spoke with Capt. Salim after moving to Atlanta, from Las Vegas in 2009 and hearing he was in the hospital undergoing surgery. When I got in contact with him he was waiting to be discharged and for his wife (Sis. Irene) to pick him up from the hospital. We spoke for about 40-45 minutes and I assured him I had not let go of the plow and how I had the blessing of being able to finally teach military science in Las Vegas and also Atlanta. The next time I heard anything was a text from Bro. Roshon out of Charlotte, North Carolina, telling me that Capt. Salim was back in the hospital and his condition wasn't good. I called Bro. Adimah Muhammad and told him I had heard that Bro. Captain was back in the hospital, and Bro. Adimah responded, "No brother, ahk is no longer with us." A ton of bricks felt like it hit my heart at this moment and I was consumed with grief. What hurt even more was the fact that I had just relocated that year and started a new job so financially I wasn't going to be able to afford time off work in addition to an airplane ticket. It was at this point a couple of days later that Bro. Roshon and I spoke and he inquired as to whether I would be attending Capt. Salim's janazah service in Phoenix, Arizona. I informed him that I couldn't afford to, he asked me if I could afford it or a way was made for me would I go then, and I responded emphatically "yes." Bro. Roshon reminded me that I had helped him and looked out for him in the past when we were in San Diego together and this would be his opportunity to pay me back, so to speak. And so, my brother, Roshon, paid my air fare for me to attend Capt. Salim's janazah and pay my respects to that mighty soldier. That's part of that brotherhood that Capt. Salim represented (thank you again Bro. Roshon). And I would like to end this with a recap of the words expressed by the Hon. Louis Farrakhan at that service:

"How should we view this? What attitude should we have? Our attitude should be thank you, Allah, for the days, the months, that we spent with our brother, that he spent with us. Thank you, Allah, for the lessons that he taught us all, thank you."

And at the Repast, the Hon. Louis Farrakhan stated,

"This is an extraordinary brother, and all of us are better because he came this way. So let us rejoice that we knew him. Take seriously the lessons that he taught us, and the way he lived his life in service. If we could be that way toward one another like Salim was, it will be a stronger Nation, a better Nation, a faster moving Nation."

I truly am grateful and thankful to almighty God, Allah, for the days, months, and years I was blessed to spend with Capt. Salim. And thank you for reading. May Allah bless you with hindsight, insight, and foresight, to guide you aright in the path of light.

Bro. Mikaeel D. S. Muhammad

Works Cited

Allah, a. r. (2002). *The Holy Qur'an, translated by Maulana Muhammad Ali.* Dublin, Ohio: Ahmadiyyah Anjuman Isha'at Islam Lahor Inc., U.S.A.

Army, D. o. (2004). *U.S. Army Counterguerrilla Operations Handbook.* Guilford, Connecticut: The Lyons Press.

Army, U. (n.d.). *U.S. Army Survival Manual FM 21-76, reprint of the Army Field Manual.* Barnes & Noble Inc. by arrangement with Platinum Press, Inc.

Butler, M. G. (1935). *War Is A Racket.* Port Townsend, Washington: The Butler Family/Feral House.

Clausewitz, C. V. (n.d.). *On War.* New York, London, Toronto: Alfred A. Knopf, edited and translated by Michael Howard and Peter Paret.

Craighead, F. C. (1943). *How to Survive on Land and Sea.* Annapolis, Maryland: Naval Institute Press.

Farrakhan, H. L. (1983). *The Meaning of F.O.I.* The Hon. Elijah Muhammad Educational Foundation/The Final Call Inc.

Force, D. o. (2003). *U.S. Air Force Search and Rescue Survival Training - AF Reg 64-4, reprint of the Air Force Field Manual.* New York: Barnes & Noble Inc.

Hill, N. (1928). *The Law of Success.* New York: Penguin Group (USA) Inc.

Hill, N. (1948). *Think Your Way To Wealth.* New York: Penguin Group (USA) Inc.

Hill, N. (2011). *Outwitting the Devil: The Secret to Freedom and Success.* New York: Sterling Publishing, The Napoleon Hill Foundation.

Muhammad, H. E. (1965). *Message to the Blackman in America.* Chicago: Muhammad's Temple No. 2, The Final Call, Inc.

Muhammad, M. F. ((original 1934), 1993). *The Supreme Wisdom.* Chicago: The Final Call, Publishers.

Renatus, F. V. (1985). *De Re Militari, translated from Latin by Lt. John Clarke (as presented in 'Roots of Strategy: The 5 Greatest Military Classics of All Time' - edited by Brig. Gen. Thomas Phillips, US Army).* Stackpole Books.

Rivero, M. (1994-2012). *What Really Happened.* Retrieved from whatreallyhappened.com: http://whatreallyhappened.com/RANCHO/POLITICS/COINTELPRO/COINTELPRO-FBI.docs.html

Seldes, G. (1947). *1000 Americans: The Real Rulers of the U.S.A.* New York: Boni & Gaer.

Sun Tzu, t. b. (1988). *The Art of War.* Boston, London: Shambhala.

USMC. (n.d.). *Drill and Ceremonies Manual.* Arlington, Virgina: Marine Corps Institute.

What is the meaning of F.O.I.?

Fruit of Islam. The name given to the military training of the men who belong to Islam in North America. – Supreme Wisdom Lost-Found Muslim Lesson No. 1 Q&A 12

"From the standpoint of society, the world may be divided into leaders and followers. The professions have their leaders, the financial world has its leaders. In all this leadership it is difficult, if not impossible, to separate from the element of pure leadership that selfish element of personal gain or advantage to the individual, without which any leadership would lose its value.

It is in military service only, where men freely sacrifice their lives for a faith, where men are willing to suffer and die for the right or prevention of a wrong, that we can hope to realize leadership in its most exalted and disinterested sense. Therefore, when I say leadership I mean military leadership."

– Major C. A. Bach (c. WWI), as printed in *'The Law of Success'* by N. Hill, pg 186

"In the F.O.I. we must teach every brother how to handle himself as a soldier and how to handle the word of God as an instrument by which the people can be saved."

– Hon. Louis Farrakhan, *The Meaning of F.O.I.*, pg 12

About the Author

Mikaeel DeWan Shabazz Muhammad was born and raised in Washington, D.C. A graduate of William McKinley H.S. aka "Tech", he was first exposed to military science in the Navy Junior Reserve Officer Training Corps (NJROTC) under the direction of Master Gunnery Sergeant Charles Washington (USMC, Ret.). Both of his grandfathers were veterans of the U.S. Air Force and Army, respectively, and his father was a veteran of the U.S. Navy. Himself a veteran of the U.S. Marine Corps graduating platoon 'Honorman' from basic training, 1st in his class at the School of Communications with a meritorious promotion, and served as an NCO, basic infantryman, radio operator/wireman, and Communications Instructor.

Intending to make the military his life-long career and eventually become an officer, those convictions changed after hearing the Hon. Louis Farrakhan speak live at the Los Angeles Coliseum in December of 1990. He later filed 'Conscientious Objector' status. He was granted said status with a General Discharge Under Honorable Conditions after being found sincere in his convictions as a Muslim and follower of the teachings of the Most Hon. Elijah Muhammad and the Hon. Louis Farrakhan.

Training in the martial arts and sciences for over 30 years, he is currently ranked 5th degree blackbelt (master) under Sijo Saabir Muhammad (fka Steve Sanders), who is the co-founder of the Black Karate Federation (BKF) and legitimately recognized founder of his own effective fighting system of Wu Shur Shin Chuan-Fa (Fist Law of the Warrior Spirit). 'Shihan' Mikaeel is also ranked 4th degree (Yondan) blackbelt in three other systems (Okinawan Kenpo, Kobujitsu, and Shotokan Karate-do) under Hanshi Tyrone Sheriff. An avid reader, martial arts instructor, writer, husband to his wife Stephanie, and father to five children, Kanisha, India, Chandany, Naadiyah, and Isaiah.

His professional service includes security, chauffeur, and executive protection specialist for numerous entertainers and VIPs. He continues to study and train as a "master student" of military and martial science.

Made in the USA
Monee, IL
04 October 2020